Schumpeter in the History of Ideas

Schumpeter in the History of Ideas

Edited by
Yuichi Shionoya and Mark Perlman

Ann Arbor
THE UNIVERSITY OF MICHIGAN PRESS

Copyright © by the University of Michigan 1994
All rights reserved
Published in the United States of America by
The University of Michigan Press
Manufactured in the United States of America
⊗Printed on acid-free paper

1997   1996   1995   1994   4   3   2   1

A CIP catalogue record for this book is available from the British Library.

Library of Congress Cataloging-in-Publication Data

Schumpeter in the history of ideas / edited by Yuichi Shionoya and Mark
    Perlman.
        p.   cm.
    Includes bibliographical references and index.
    ISBN 0-472-10548-5 (alk. paper)
    1. Schumpeter, Joseph Alois, 1883–1950—Congresses. 2. Economics—
History—20th century—Congresses.   I. Shionoya, Yuichi, 1932–
II. Perlman, Mark.
HB119.S35S377   1994
330′.092—dc20   94-34016
                                                                               CIP

Contents

Introduction

The fourth biennial meeting of the International Schumpeter Society was held in Kyoto in August, 1992. The participants were 130 economists from twenty countries, and fifty papers were presented under the overall theme "Innovation in Technology, Industries, and Institutions: Comparative Perspectives." From among the papers delivered to this meeting, we have edited two volumes: one for innovation and the other for Schumpeter's thought. The first is titled *Innovation in Technology, Industries, and Institutions: Studies in Schumpeterian Perspective*. The second is the present volume, titled *Schumpeter in the History of Ideas*.

The International Schumpeter Society was founded in 1986 with the aim of promoting the scientific study of the problems of economic development and innovation along the lines suggested by Joseph Alois Schumpeter. Thus, the first through third biennial conferences of the Society were largely concerned with the themes in the Schumpeterian tradition, such as technological innovation, entrepreneurship, market structure, and economic development. Although these themes were still the core subject of discussion in the fourth conference, we planned to discuss, in addition, several new topics that were related to Schumpeter's economic and social thought. Discussions of this sort are valuable and help us understand the total background of Schumpeter's ideas and his framework of analysis. The present volume is the result of such a program.

Concurrently with this conference, the year 1992 was the 50th anniversary of the publication of Schumpeter's *Capitalism, Socialism and Democracy*. Concern for the gigantic problems of the transformation of economic and political systems has been growing in the face of the restructuring of the post-Communist systems. Schumpeter's thought about the fate of capitalism is, in a deeper sense, still relevant to the world situation that emerged after his death—namely, the growth of capitalism in the United States, Europe, and Japan, on the one hand, and the breakdown of Communism in Central and Eastern Europe, on the other. The implications of his thought and vision can be developed and interpreted in the context of the present world. This task will be fruitfully fulfilled on the basis of the clear understanding of his many-faceted ideas and their origins. Here lies a strong temptation to look at Schumpeter in the history of thought.

At the Kyoto meeting of the Society, the 1992 Schumpeter Prize was awarded to Richard A. Musgrave (Harvard University) and Christopher Green (McGill University). The prize competition theme was "Government, the 'Tax State' and Economic Dynamics." Needless to say, the theme refers to Schumpeter's book, *The Crisis of the Tax State,* published in 1918. Schumpeter's central idea about the fate of capitalism, which was fully developed in his book of 1942, was first presented in a seminal form in his book of 1918. His famous vision of a capitalist system destroying itself by its forces of development from within was clearly presented there in an enlarged context of socioeconomics or economic sociology. By the crisis of the tax state, he meant nothing less than the transformation of the capitalist system, because it had come to place a growing emphasis on public expenditure and social control. The essays of Musgrave and Green were published in *Journal of Evolutionary Economics,* Vol. 2, No. 2, 1992, and Vol. 3, No. 1, 1993. Shigeto Tsuru delivered the Schumpeter Lecture on "If Schumpeter Were Alive Today" at the Schumpeter Prize Banquet. His essay is published in the present volume.

The Schumpeter Prize and the banquet were donated by the German economic weekly magazine *Wirtschaftswoche.* We express appreciation to *Wirtschaftswoche* for their generosity, which has invariably been paid to Schumpeter and Schumpeterians from the time of their former *Der deutsche Volkswirt.* We are indebted, further, to many Japanese business firms for their financial assistance, without which the Kyoto conference and the publication of its results would not have been realized.

In the introductory essay to this volume, Shigeto Tsuru asks his readers to ponder the current economic debate "If Schumpeter Were Alive Today." Tsuru believes that Schumpeter would regard the Japanese economic "miracle" as an empirical confirmation of his thesis of "creative destruction," and, further, speculates that Schumpeter may well have regarded the current trend toward conglomeration and privatization as evidence of the succession of capitalism by a form of socialism.

Erich Streissler attempts to explore the roots of Schumpeter's economic thought in "The Influence of German and Austrian Economics on Joseph A. Schumpeter." Streissler argues that Schumpeter's genius lay not in his innovative theories, but, rather, in the manner in which he wove the themes already present in German and Austrian economics into the fabric of neoclassical theory. While Schumpeter appears as somewhat of an anomaly to Anglo-American economists, he is seen as being "at home" in the German-Austrian tradition.

Kiichiro Yagi principally questions Streissler's characterization of Schumpeter as an individualist, noting the tension between individualism and *methodological* individualism. He also asserts a tension between such labels as individualist and subjectivist.

"Joseph Schumpeter: Radical Economist" is Nathan Rosenberg's estimation of Schumpeter as critic of neoclassical theory. Rosenberg asserts that *Capitalism, Socialism and Democracy* is a treatise on change, and, as such, is in direct contrast to the Walrasian general equilibrium paradigm, which is characterized as static and concerned with equilibrium states. Change and dynamics are the central constituents of Schumpeter's work; capitalism is evolutionary; everything matters and so is endogenous. This view led Schumpeter to reject formalism in favor of historical analysis of the changing dynamics of society.

Laurence Moss considers Rosenberg's analysis of the milieu within which Schumpeter came to the questions discussed in *Capitalism, Socialism and Democracy*. Moss sees Schumpeter's originality as somewhat overstated by Rosenberg. He also notes inconsistencies in Schumpeter's price theory, specifically in whether competition is a "discovery" procedure or an axiom necessary to the functioning of the theoretical model, and expresses disappointment that the issue of technological change was not more fully explored by Rosenberg.

Jürgen Backhaus investigates "The Concept of the Tax State in Modern Public Finance Analysis." He suggests that, throughout Schumpeter's work, the "tax state" appears as a central concept, not confined, as in much of the modern public finance literature, to theoretical models. It is as well applicable to empirical (historical) analyses of real-world economies.

The relation between Schumpeter and John Maynard Keynes is the topic of C. W. A. M. van Paridon's "Schumpeter and Keynes: An Early Confrontation." The confrontation centered on the question of the gold standard, with Schumpeter (in a companion article to this contribution, published in Dutch in 1925) arguing in favor of the policy, in opposition to the well-known critique presented by Keynes. It is readily apparent that the two were arguing from different perspectives, statics versus dynamics, short-run versus long-run, formalism versus historical analysis, consumption versus entrepreneurial innovation, to name just a few.

Commenting on the paper, and the Schumpeter contribution, Mark Perlman believes that more of the intellectual development of Schumpeter's thesis, as well as a taste for the rhetoric employed in promoting the thesis, should have been explored. One of Schumpeter's difficulties was his need never to suffer equals.

If Schumpeter Were Alive Today

Shigeto Tsuru

If Schumpeter were alive today, it is certain that he would have joined us here in Kyoto with zest. For one thing, he would have wished to revisit the temples and the Nijo Palace, which were the objects of his artistic admiration sixty-one years ago, when he visited the city for the first time, and for whose survival he feared during their wartime bombard-ment.[1] In particular, he would wish to confirm his on-the-spot judgment, in 1931, that one of the screen-panels in the Nishi-Honganji Temple was not by the same Kanō School artist as the other panels, although Profes-sor Yasuma Takata, who guided him there, insisted it was. Later, after Schumpeter had left Japan, it was confirmed by a Kanō School expert that Schumpeter was correct in his judgment.

Most of you probably know that Schumpeter once told Theodore Morgan that, other than the three well-known ambitions of his life—to be the greatest lover in Vienna, the greatest horseman in Europe, and the greatest economist in the world—there were two more ambitions, one of which was to be an accomplished connoisseur of art.[2] Not only was Schumpeter a connoisseur of French architecture, but we can testify to the fact that he had a unique aesthetic sense, to also appreciate the objects of fine art in the category of classical Japanese painting.

The city of Kyoto would also bring to him another of his cherished memories. Guiding Schumpeter during his Kyoto tour were Professor Takata and a young instructor, Kei Shibata. Shibata had just published an article in which he questioned the theoretical consistency of Gustav Cassel's system of general equilibrium equations. He was, furthermore, in the process of trying to combine the Walrasian system with the Marx-ian reproduction scheme, an attempt which was later to be published in

---

1. Robert Loring Allen, *Opening Doors* (New Brunswick: Transaction Publishers, 1991), 2:138.

2. Theodore Morgan's letter to *The Economist,* 24 December 1983, quoted in Rich-ard Swedberg, *Joseph A. Schumpeter—His Life and Work* (Cambridge: Polity Press, 1991), 46.

the *Kyoto University Economic Review* (July 1933), and which was to immediately attract the attention of Oskar Lange. Schumpeter was naturally impressed by the scientific talent of this young instructor at Kyoto University and anticipated a promising future for Shibata as an economic scientist. Probably far more than to any other visiting Japanese economist, Schumpeter shared his time generously in consultation with Shibata, during the latter's sojourn in Cambridge, in 1936. If the two could meet here today, the occasion would be one of happy reunion for them. I know that Schumpeter harbored special affection for the academic atmosphere of Kyoto.

If Schumpeter were alive today, there is one thing that I am pretty certain he would have asserted. We all know of his concept of "creative destruction." He wrote, in his *Capitalism, Socialism, and Democracy:* "This process of Creative Destruction is the essential fact about capitalism. It is what capitalism consists in and what every capitalist enterprise has got to live in."[3] "Through destruction capitalism creates anew" was his theme, and he used to say that the Great Kanto Earthquake of 1923 provided an exceptional occasion in Japan for economic prosperity, characterized by creative responses of all kinds.

If Schumpeter were alive today, he would comment on the aftermath of the extraordinary degree of destruction and devastation that were the consequences of the war in Japan. He would note that the Japanese economy, essentially capitalistic, surpassed all expectations in the immediate postwar years by growing, during the decades of the 1950s and 1960s, at a cumulative annual rate of almost ten percent, in real GNP. Was this, then, a case of creative destruction?

As a matter of fact, Kenneth Boulding, apparently alluding to the Schumpeterian concept of "creative destruction," advanced a hypothesis of "creative defeat," saying that "very often there is the creative reaction to defeat; Japan is an example of a fantastically creative response to defeat."[4] A question comes to our mind immediately: why was it that after the First World War, Germany, as mature a capitalist society as Japan was in the 1940s, could not display this creative response to defeat? Schumpeter provided an answer to this question, though indirectly, when he wrote in his *Die Krise des Steuerstaates* that it would take an eloquent and dynamic leader with a strong and unified government

---

3. J. A. Schumpeter, *Capitalism, Socialism, and Democracy,* 3d ed. (New York: Harper Brothers Publishers, 1950), 83.
4. Kenneth E. Boulding, in his address to a Foreign Relations Dinner held at the International House of Japan, 30 January 1984, reproduced in *IHJ Bulletin* 4 (2 Spring 1984): 2.

behind him to succeed in the postwar recovery. It is clear enough that Germany at that time lacked such a leader, and that the Ebert government was not such a government. Also, Schumpeter wrote elsewhere,[5] using the example of an economy devastated by war, that if only buildings and material objects have been destroyed, the damage is not irreparable; as long as the authority structure and the general organization of the economy are intact, the economy will soon be running at full speed again.

If Schumpeter were alive today, I surmise that he could claim that Japan's "fantastically creative response to defeat" was nothing but a concrete illustration of his pet thesis of "creative destruction," on a grand scale. He would point to the unified autonomy of the Supreme Commander of the Allied Powers, which forcefully maintained the general organization of the Japanese economy for as long as seven years under paternalistic occupation.

Still, something more than this was required for Japan's capitalism to display a model case of either creative destruction or creative defeat. Most important in this connection was, beyond doubt, the availability of forward-looking entrepreneurship—another uniquely Schumpeterian concept in the theory of economic development. On this concept of entrepreneurship, however, we know that Schumpeter gradually changed his ideas, as he began to lay greater stress on empirical studies in economic history, in the 1930s and 1940s. In a word, he no longer thought the entrepreneurial function had to be embodied in a physical person. In other words, a collection of individuals or a whole team could be "the entrepreneur"; and even the state could play its role.[6] I believe that in the background of such an evolution of ideas on the part of Schumpeter was the recognition that huge corporations, through their giant research and development departments, were becoming more and more successful in eliminating the need for the individual innovator, as was exemplified by the development of nylon by DuPont Co. in 1937, replacing the U.S. import need for raw silk from Japan.

In the case of postwar Japan, Schumpeter's matured conception of the entrepreneurial function was well enough confirmed through the innovational activities of teams of researchers hired by big (Toyota, NEC, etc.) and small (Sony, etc.) corporations, as well as through the paternalistic assistance of the state. If Schumpeter were alive today, he

---

5. In the last chapter, entitled: "The Overall Picture of the Economy" of *Theorie der wirtschaftlichen Entwicklung* (first edition, 1911), the chapter which was omitted in the second edition. See Swedberg, *op. cit.,* 38.

6. Swedberg, *Joseph A. Schumpeter,* 171–73.

would say that he was vindicated in his matured theoretical judgment through the experience of Japan.

If Schumpeter were alive today, the biggest and most controversial problem he would have to confront would be his vision as regards the fate of capitalism.

As we all know, Schumpeter believed in the effectiveness of the objective law of socioeconomic development, or *objektive gesellschaftliche Gesetzmassigkeit.* He wrote, for example:

> Things economic and social move by their own momentum and the ensuing situations compel individuals and groups to behave in certain ways whatever they may wish to do—not indeed by destroying their freedom of choice but by shaping the choosing mentalities and by narrowing the list of possibilities from which to choose.[7]

And more specifically, referring to the fate of capitalism, he wrote:

> The capitalist process not only destroys its own institutional framework but it also creates the conditions for another. Destruction may not be the right word after all. Perhaps I should have spoken of transformation. The outcome of the process is not simply a void that could be filled by whatever might happen to turn up; things and souls are transformed in such a way as to become increasingly amenable to the socialist form of life. With every peg from under the capitalist structure vanishes an impossibility of the socialist plan.[8]

It is revealing to note that Schumpeter added a comment, immediately following the sentence I have just quoted, to the effect that, in this respect, "Marx's *vision* was right."

A crucial question, or a "sixty-four dollar question" in the prewar jargon of Americans, we can and should ask Schumpeter today would be: How would he square the postwar developments of capitalism *and* socialism with his erstwhile vision and analysis?

I do not have to dwell upon the plain-enough facts that can be observed in the world during the last four decades; namely: the rejuvenation of capitalism cum the spreading of privatization, and the disintegration of major socialist countries cum the attempt to introduce market principles in them.

---

7. Schumpeter, *Capitalism, Socialism, and Democracy,* 129–30.
8. Ibid., 162.

The highlight of this double-faceted worldwide trend was an international conference on privatization sponsored by the United States Agency for International Development (USAID), held in Washington, D.C., in February, 1986, where nearly five hundred delegates from forty-six countries assembled. They were addressed by Secretary of State George P. Schultz, who explained that the conference symbolized a "revolution in economic thinking. It has been an unusual revolution in that it is a return to principles we once adhered to, but from which we had strayed. They are principles of individual freedom and private enterprise that have changed the world more in 200 years than all the changes in the preceding 2,000 years."[9]

What might Schumpeter say to this type of statement, if he were alive today? Before I try to speculate on his likely answer to this question, I propose to confirm his position on socialism. As Robert Loring Allen wrote: "Schumpeter defined socialism as a system requiring a central authority to control the means of production and the production process."[10] Further, Schumpeter argued that socialism could be a logical system with the parametric use of prices to achieve market equilibrium, citing an early proof by Enrico Barone (1908), later depending on Oskar Lange's more sophisticated version of the subject (1937). However, it should be noted that "Schumpeter emphasized very strongly that socialism is possible only if the capitalist system has exhausted itself."[11]

Beyond making such generalized remarks on a *model* of socialist society, Schumpeter did not wrestle with the *reality* of the "socialist" societies at the time. In fact, "it took but a few sentences for him to dispose of the comparison between Soviet socialist reality and capitalist reality. In that case, capitalism won, mainly because the Russians did not follow anything even remotely resembling Schumpeter's blueprint of socialism."[12] In other words, Schumpeter did not think of the Soviet Union as a socialist country. Rather, he used the term "Russian imperialism"; and he was "very upset that while public opinion had been so quick to condemn Hitler, there was no equivalent fury over Stalin's gradual takeover of Europe."[13]

Although Schumpeter condemned Stalin's regime in much stronger terms in private conversations with us at Harvard than in published writings, he harbored warm feelings toward "intellectual socialists," like

---

9. Quoted in Steve H. Hanke, ed., *Privatization and Development* (San Francisco: Institute of Contemporary Studies, 1987), 17–18.

10. Allen, *Opening Doors*, 2:126.

11. Swedberg, *Joseph A. Schumpeter*, 159.

12. Allen, *Opening Doors*, 128–29.

13. Swedberg, *Joseph A. Schumpeter*, 170.

Paul Sweezy and myself; and he even called Paul Samuelson "a socialist" to his face on one occasion, and against Paul's protest, made a remark: "My dear Paul, I was merely making reference to what you will not deny, that you lack respect for the pietistic verities of capitalism."[14]

So much for Schumpeter's socialism. And now we come to what is likely to be a most controversial question, and that is: In the light of what transpired among advanced capitalist economies during the past forty years, is there not a need for a revision of the earlier vision of the fate of capitalism on the part of Schumpeter?

It is true that capitalism, in general, displayed a degree of success that went beyond the expectations of a large number of economists. But one inevitably recalls here the oft-quoted remark by Schumpeter: "In the end there is not so much difference as one might think between saying that the decay of capitalism is due to its success and saying that it is due to its failure."[15] The meaning of this somewhat paradoxical statement is usually understood in the form of what is known as "the Schumpeterian hypothesis," to the effect "(1) that innovations tend to be more frequent in monopolistic industries than in competitive ones; and (2) that large firms are more innovative than small ones."[16] In this way, capitalist enterprises, increasingly "trustified" (in Schumpeter's terminology), tend to make progress routine, and thus "capitalism itself renders capitalism superfluous."[17] In the process of such an evolutionary trend of capitalism, Schumpeter believed that control and decision making would gradually change from private to public hands; and if people still wanted to call the system by such terms as "guided capitalism" or "mixed economy," he would say that it was a matter of taste, and concede that then you could say that what you prefer to call "capitalism" might progress and survive longer.

There remains the question of privatization, for which Mrs. Thatcher's government of Great Britain became the trendsetter after her election victory in May 1979. Does this trend contradict Schumpeter's vision of the fate of capitalism? I do not think so. I shall not spend much time on this complex problem here, but it is important to note that the dichotomy in ownership (private versus public) is not parallel with the dichotomy in market relations (competition versus monopoly). Thus, in Britain's case, according to the assessment by Vickers and Yarrow,

---

14. Paul A. Samuelson, "The World Economy at Century's End," paper presented at the World Economic Conference, Mexico City, Mexico, 1980, 20–21.

15. Schumpeter, *Capitalism, Socialism, and Democracy,* 162.

16. Swedburg, *Joseph A. Schumpeter,* 157.

17. Allen, *Opening Doors,* 2:125.

whereas in markets where effective (actual or potential) competition, such as Amersham, British Aerospace, or Enterprise Oil prevailed, it was found that private ownership—hence privatization—was efficient and suitable, "policy dilemmas became sharper when the Government's ambition to privatize grew to embrace firms with extensive market power. Where monopoly exists—that 'great enemy to good management' in Adam Smith's words—the case for preferring private ownership to public ownership weakens considerably: privately efficient profit seeking can no longer be expected to lead to socially efficient results."[18]

In conclusion, we may concur with Allen, when he writes: "Most economists are not prepared to write off capitalism, but many would add the word 'yet'. Schumpeter put no firm date on the succession of socialism and even waffled on just what constituted socialism. Certainly, many of the elements that he argued were undermining capitalism and favoring socialism are still at work and may one day bring the predominance of the public economy. And perhaps, as time passes, we will change our mind as to what constitutes capitalism and socialism, calling one the other."[19] I suspect Schumpeter would agree with this, if he were here today.

Lastly, we come to the problem of "Schumpeter as a scientist." We have assembled here in a large number as either students or followers of Schumpeter, but not necessarily in the form of the Schumpeterian School. In fact, we should say that there is no such thing as "the Schumpeterian School," as there are "the Keynesian School" or "the Marxian School." It was Schumpeter, himself, who wrote that "schools have no place in economics. If economics is a science and if economists are scientists, then each contributor is a bit player and makes only a small contribution."[20]

It happens that this remark is in accord with how Professors Takata and Shibata of Kyoto University conceived of their life-long mission as economic scientists, as they were wont to cite Akiko Yosano's poem: "For the sanctuary, conceived since the eternal past, I, for one, add a golden nail." (*Gōsho yori tsukuri-itonamu dendo ni, ware wa ōgon no kugi hitotsu utsu.*) It is because of this coincidental rapport on the mission of a scientist that Schumpeter harbored, as I remarked earlier, special affection for the academic atmosphere of Kyoto.

Nevertheless, we must raise a problem here: economic phenomena,

---

18. John Vickers and George Yarrow, *Privatization—An Economic Analysis* (Cambridge, Mass.: MIT Press, 1988), 426.

19. Allen, *Opening Doors,* 2:261.

20. Ibid., 272.

unlike natural objects of study, are bound to evolve as time goes on and to continue to present to us new types of problems, which were not part of the objects of analysis in earlier periods. "The sanctuary conceived since the eternal past" in Akiko's simile is not adequate for economic science. It requires constant redesigning and major alterations. Schumpeter was perfectly aware of this; and thus was born his theory of economic development.

Furthermore, as Marx would have said that "one gains freedom through insight into necessity," objective laws in economics, unlike those in natural science, are subject to modification through conscious action by human agents, who have discerned them and who have set out to accomplish certain goals. Although Schumpeter agreed with Hilferding in thinking that to prove the necessity does not mean that one desires for its realization, he could not deny the therapeutic, or positively reforming, function of political economy.

In spite of these reminders, however, Schumpeter continued to seek, I believe, an elegant purity of economic science, for which he considered Quesnay, Cournot, and Walras to have been the greatest contributors in the past. He repeated, time and again, the statement that "the highest ambition an economist can entertain who believes in the scientific character of economics would be fulfilled as soon as he succeeded in constructing a simple model displaying all the essential features of the economic process by means of a reasonably small number of equations connecting a reasonably small number of variables. Work on this line is laying the foundation of the economics of the future and should command the highest respect of all of us."[21]

It is clear that Schumpeter did not achieve this ambition. I suspect, however, that the persevering effort with which he tried to master mathematics, and the repeated mention of planning to write, in cooperation with Georgescu-Roegen, a conspectus on the theoretical apparatus of economic science, toward the end of his life, must have been the evidence of his continued striving in the direction of fulfilling his ambition. If Schumpeter had lived longer, it is possible that we could have celebrated, on this occasion, the crowning achievement of his career. Who among us could follow his footsteps in this endeavor?

---

21. J. Schumpeter, "The American Economy in the Interwar Period—The Decade of the Twenties," *American Economic Review*, Proceedings, May 1946, 3.

The Influence of German and Austrian Economics on Joseph A. Schumpeter

Erich W. Streissler

Ich las und wurde überzeugt, daß die Gesellschaft den großen Mann bilden muß, bevor er sie neubilden kann, so daß alle jene Veränderungen, deren nächster Urheber er ist, ihre Hauptursache in den Generationen haben, von denen er abstammt.

[I read and was convinced that society must shape the great man before he can shape it anew, so that all the changes of which he is the proximate author have their main cause in the generations from which he springs.]

—Friedrich Freiherr von Wieser

1

We have heard it repeated time and again that Joseph A. Schumpeter was a man unusually widely read in the history of economic thought, in fact in the history of all the humanities. Rarely, however, does somebody draw the obvious conclusion that what he had read must have strongly influenced, if not largely conditioned the man both in his themes and in his modes of thinking.

The neglect of Schumpeter's roots in the history of thought is in itself a facet of this very history of thought: Schumpeter's mind was in its formative stages when the vision of the scientist or the artist as superman in the mold of Friedrich Nietzsche, a superman spurning and flaunting his environment, was most prevalent in German and Austrian intellectual life; and Swedberg[1] shows that Schumpeter tried to model himself on Nietzsche's precepts. Haberler voiced this heroic view in his obituary of

---

1. Richard Swedberg, *Joseph A. Schumpeter—His Life and Work* (Cambridge: Polity Press, 1991). Swedberg summarizes on page 192: "To some extent one can say that Schumpeter lived in a similar universe to that of the German philosopher . . . Nietzsche."

Schumpeter when he quotes Nietzsche: "Seht ihn nur an—Niemandem war er untertan" [Just look at him, he was subservient to none].[2]

Yet one has to remember that in the course of the training of an academic economist in Vienna around the turn of the century the young acolyte for the "Habilitation" was required to read a hundred odd books, stretching in time of publication over the whole preceding century; and that the examiners expected him, above all, to be thoroughly versed in German and Austrian economic literature. And it is in this literature that all of Schumpeter's themes can be found. Schumpeter *was* highly original. This originality, however, lies not in the topics he introduced into mainstream economics, but rather in the novel twists he gave to these themes, on the one hand, and on the other hand, in the new mixture of and the new insistence on these themes, modifications that transformed them into a much stronger brew. It was *not* the by then belaboured theme of German economic literature, the figure of the creative entrepreneur, that was new in Schumpeter, but rather the idea of creative destruction by entrepreneurial innovation. It was *not* the well-worn German idea of the importance of bank credit for economic development that was new, but rather Schumpeter's notion that bank credit was the prerequisite of innovation and of the foundation of new enterprises—by the way a novel theoretical idea of Schumpeter's that is palpably wrong.[3] New also was the notion that inflation stimulated growth and innovation, a notion still very controversial and, in fact, much in doubt. It was not Schumpeter's stress on the importance of monopoly that was new, but in a measure his view that monopolies were engines of growth.

I have repeatedly pointed out how deeply the Austrian School of economics—from its founder, Carl Menger, onward—was rooted in an older "protoneoclassical" German economic tradition prevalent during the first three quarters of the nineteenth century.[4] In part 2 of this paper, I

---

2. Gottfried von Haberler, "Joseph Alois Schumpeter 1883–1950," *Quarterly Journal of Economics* LXIV (1950): 333, 344. Haberler says: "His independence was not a pose. One could truly say of him what Nietzsche said of Schopenhauer" and then adds the verse quoted above. He says: "His ideas . . . are . . . supremely independent of his scientific environment."

3. See Erich Streissler, "Schumpeter's Vienna and the Role of Credit in Innovation," in *Schumpeterian Economics,* ed. Helmut Frisch (Eastbourne, N.Y.: Praeger, 1981), 60 ff., 74 ff.

4. See Erich W. Streissler, "The Influence of German Economics on the Work of Menger and Marshall," *History of Political Economy* 22 (suppl., 1990a): 31 ff.; Erich Streissler, "Carl Menger, der deutsche Nationalökonom," in *Studien zur Entwicklung der ökonomischen Theorie,* Vol. 10, ed. Bertram Schefold, Schriften des Vereins für Socialpolitik, N.F. vol.115/X (Berlin: Duncker und Humblot, 1990b), 153 ff.

shall give an outline of this sophisticated theory of the entrepreneur in this German tradition and indicate the ideas that Schumpeter found there, ready for him to use. In part 3, I shall turn to the German insistence on the importance of banking and credit and to the consequences of this for Schumpeter's thought. Part 4 will examine traditional German and Austrian ideas about monopolies and big business and their beneficial effects—ideas in sharp contrast to Anglo-American skepticism about monopolies. Part 5 will examine the obvious connection of Schumpeter's (and all the later Austrians') ideas on the effects of credit and, in the case of Schumpeter, on monopolies with German Marxist literature, in particular with Rudolf Hilferding's *Finanzkapital*. Part 6 is to show that Schumpeter's ideas on statics and dynamics are but a variation on his teacher, Friedrich von Wieser's, original treatment of these economic themes. Today's Neo-Austrians usually do not regard Schumpeter as a member of the Austrian School of economics. The concluding part 7 of this paper will therefore outline his close connection with the Austrians' "subjective value." As is well known, the Austrian School clashed with the younger German Historical School of Gustav von Schmoller from the 1880s onward. Here, Schumpeter, tried to take a middle position: As Swedberg points out, Schumpeter, in an extensive essay, found favorable words on Schmoller;[5] and, of course, Schumpeter himself became a German professor for several years (at Bonn, 1925—1932). But, in particular, his program for a "social" economics was close to that of Max Weber, the German economist and sociologist who tried to bridge the conflict of the Historical School and the more theoretical Austrians. This German connection will also be remarked upon in part 7.

2

German economics of the nineteenth century never lost touch with the literature of high mercantilism and the analysis of the entrepreneurial role (or more properly the role of the "merchant") presented there, while this contact was lost in the English economic literature after Adam Smith's strictures on the "mercantile system," a system that Smith both condemned and denigrated, or, rather, ridiculed as to its intellectual content. In the very beginning of his fundamental treatise, Mun already had extensively discussed the informational role of the

---

5. See Swedberg, *Life and Work*, 66, 98, 107. The article was Joseph A. Schumpeter, "Gustav von Schmoller und die Probleme von heute," *Schmollers Jahrbuch für Gesetzgebung, Verwaltung und Volkswirtschaft* 50 (1926): 337–88. Notice that this was published only after Schumpeter had become a German professor in Bonn.

merchant, and Cantillon had written at length on his risk-taking role. This tradition was partly continued by Jean Baptiste Say,[6] an author very influential in the western parts of Germany during the first quarter of the nineteenth century, a region that was for some time under French political and much more so under French intellectual domination. The first German author of the German subjective value tradition, Gottlieb Hufeland, gave the entrepreneur a central role in his influential economic treatise of 1807,[7] which was later much quoted by Carl Menger, the founder of the Austrian School.[8] Hufeland tried to argue against the classical notion that prices were determined by cost. In fact, he said, most of the time demand prices (that are realized in the market) differ from supply prices. The demand prices are received by entrepreneurs and the difference between demand and cost-determined supply price constitutes entrepreneurial income, profit. Thus, with Hufeland, profit on average is an important component of income; but it is a *disequilibrium* income as we would say today, though Hufeland did not say it in these words. In this sense, the entrepreneur is a disequilibrium phenomenon for Hufeland more than one hundred years before Schumpeter stressed the disequilibrating or "dynamic" role of the entrepreneur.

The rather obvious point of Hufeland (interesting only because of his notion that *on average,* over time or over commodities, we must not neglect these disequilibrium profits) became important for German theory only because the most influential German textbook of the first half of the nineteenth century misunderstood it, yet gave it prominent place, and built on this misunderstanding an extensive discussion of the entrepreneurial role. The author of this central textbook, Karl Heinrich

---

6. I have discussed the history of economic ideas on the entrepreneurial role in Erich Streissler, "Der Unternehmer in der deutschen Nationalökonomie des 19. Jahrhunderts," in *Wirtschaftswachstum, Strukturwandel und dynamischer Wettbewerb,* ed. B. Gahlen et al., Ernst Helmstädter zum 65. Geburtstag (Berlin, Heidelberg: Springer, 1989), 17 ff. See Thomas Mun, *England's Treasure by Forraign Trade,* London (Thomas Clark, 1664), chap. 1; Richard Cantillon, *Essai sur la nature du commerce en général,* "Londres," 1755, book I, ch. 13; Jean Baptiste Say, *Traité d'économice politique,* ou simple exposition de la manière dont se forment, distribuent et se consomment les Richesses, 2 vol. (Paris 1803). Quoted from: *A Treatise on Political Economy,* New American Edition (Philadelphia: Claxton, 1880), book 2, ch. 7, sec. 3.

7. Gottlieb Hufeland, *Neue Grundlegung der Staatswirthschaftskunst, durch Prüfung und Berichtigung ihrer Hauptbegriffe von Gut, Werth, Preis, Geld und Volksvermögen mit ununterbrochener Rücksicht auf die bisherigen Systeme* (Giessen and Wetzlar: Tasche and Müller, 1807).

8. Carl Menger, *Grundsätze der Volkswirthschaftslehre* (Wien: Braumüller, 1871). Hufeland is quoted on pp. 2, 5, 215, and 230.

Rau,[9] thought Hufeland took the entrepreneur to be a *fourth factor of production;* though actually entrepreneurial income as a disequilibrium income is, with Hufeland, a type of income on quite a different logical level from the equilibrium incomes (rent, interest, and wages) of the permanent factors of production (land, capital, and labor).

Rau stresses that the combination of factors of production in the right proportions is a difficult undertaking: "He, who for the sake of his profit combines sources of production in such a way that they gain productive power,[10] is called the *entrepreneur of this branch of production.*" The role of the entrepreneur is not that of an owner of factors of production but that of an *intermediary* between owners, that of serving as their common *agent:* "Thus it is the entrepreneur who mediates between the owners of the sources of production."[11] Wieser's and Schumpeter's idea that the entrepreneur normally is not the final owner of his factors of production, but has usually only borrowed them,[12] is thus propounded already nearly a century before them by Rau: in the textbook, on which, according to Wieser, every German-language economist was brought up.[13] Rau goes on to say that the entrepreneurial contribution lies firstly in this *intermediation* between factor owners, secondly in the *management* of the firm ("die Leitung des Geschäftes") and thirdly and finally "usually" also in shouldering the *risk* of the enterprise.[14] For him (and most of the German authors, with the prominent exception of Mangoldt) risk bearing implies but the simple notion that the expected value of all capital gains and losses has to be at least zero: the successful ventures have to compensate for the unsuccessful ones. The tasks of management, on the other

9. Karl Heinrich Rau, *Grundsätze der Volkswirtschaftslehre* (Lehrbuch der politischen Oekonomie, Erster Band) (Leipzig und Heidelberg: 1826, 6th ed., 1855).

10. Rau, *Grundsätze,* 157, § 136: "Derjenige, welcher seines Gewinnes willen die Güterquellen miteinander in eine solche Verbindung setzt, daß sie eine hervorbringende Wirkung äußern, ist der *Unternehmer eines Productionszweiges.*"

11. Rau, *Grundsätze,* 158, § 136: "Der Unternehmer ist es also, welcher die Vermittelung zwischen den Eigenthümern der einzelnen Güterquellen . . . vornimmt."

12. Friedrich Freiherr von Wieser, *Theorie der gesellschaftlichen Wirtschaft,* Grundriss der Sozialökonomik 1/2, 2d ed. (Tübingen: J.C.B. Mohr, 1924), 251; Joseph Schumpeter, *Theorie der wirtschaftlichen Entwicklung,* Eire Untersuchung über Unternehmergewinn, Kapital, Kredit, Zins und Konjunkturzyklus, 2d ed. (Munich and Leipzig: Duncker und Humblot, 1926), 103 ff.

13. Friedrich Wieser, *Karl Menger, Neue Österreichische Biographie 1815–1918,* Vol. 1 (Vienna: 1923), 84 ff., says that Rau was the "solid" textbook "which German youths had used year after year for their education." German in the sense of 1923 includes Austrian youths.

14. Rau, *Grundsätze,* 158, § 137. ("In den meisten Fällen auch die Übernahme der Gefahr, daß das Unternehmen mißlingt oder doch nicht nach Erwartung gelingt und daß folglich das angewendete Vermögen ganz oder theilweise verlorengeht.")

hand, are elaborated in interesting detail. It is a kind of "labour, and a difficult one," demanding, as it does, "higher intellectual and moral abilities." The many tasks enumerated by Rau pertain partly to *organization* and partly to *information gathering* and its evaluation. In spite of the fact that Rau calls the entrepreneurial effort a kind of labor, he summarizes his position explicitly: "It is most appropriate to the nature of the problem to consider entrepreneurial income as a kind of income peculiar to itself, which arises out of the close combination of labour and capital and within which the part cannot be isolated which these two causes have in the common effect."[15] In the exposition of his treatise, Rau always treats entrepreneurial income as a distinctive fourth category of factor incomes.[16] Both in the assumption that the specific contribution of the entrepreneur is organization and that he constitutes a distinctive fourth factor of production, Rau, as I have pointed out elsewhere, evidently foreshadows Alfred Marshall, who read Rau early in his career as an economist.[17]

In his ideas on the role of the entrepreneur, Rau, thus, is actually a precursor of Marshall, rather than of Schumpeter. He is important for Schumpeterian thought only in three respects: first of all, for inaugurating the tradition that German economic textbooks from his time onward tended to discuss the economic role of the entrepreneur extensively; secondly by considering the entrepreneur, as Schumpeter always does, as an economic agent quite distinct from the capitalist; and thirdly by contributing to the subsequent Schumpeterian standard phrase, namely that the entrepreneur seeks out "new combinations," the notion behind the noun, the distinctive need for *combining* factors of production appropriately. But the notion behind the perhaps more important adjective "new" in this phrase is totally lacking in Rau.

In the later standard German textbook tradition, as represented by Wilhelm Roscher,[18] Rau's ideas merged into the catchy phrase that the entrepreneur provides "*Organisation, Speculation* und *Inspection,*" these German terms being immediately understandable to the English reader.

---

15. Rau, *Grundsätze,* 258, § 238: "Es ist dem Wesen der Sache am meisten angemessen, den Gewerbsverdienst als ein eigenthümliches Einkommen anzusehen, welches aus der innigen Verbindung der Arbeit und des Capitales entspringt und in welchem der Antheil nicht auszuscheiden ist, den jede dieser beiden Ursachen an ihrer gemeinschaftlichen Wirkung hat".

16. Rau, *Grundsätze,* 160, § 139, 294–303, § 237–44.

17. On the relationship of Marshall to Rau, see Streissler, *Influence,* 55 ff., especially 56.

18. Wilhelm Roscher, *Die Grundlagen der Nationalökonomie,* 6th ed., book III, chap. 5 (Stuttgart: Cotta, 1864), 401, § 195.

From reading Roscher one gathers that the phrase is not actually his, but was coined by the Prussian economist Riedel, who published a textbook on economics in Berlin in 1838.[19] Riedel was well known thirty-five or seventy years later in the Austrian School, being, for example, quoted in Menger's "Principles."[20] This is perhaps best proved by the fact that the copy of Riedel's textbook in the library of the Institute of Economics of the University of Vienna that I used bears the ex libris "Dr. Eugen Böhm, Universitäts-Professor"; in other words, it was the personal copy of Schumpeter's teacher, Böhm-Bawerk. It is nearly certain that Schumpeter was throroughly familiar with Riedel, though as usual we have the difficulty that in contrast to Menger and Böhm-Bawerk, Schumpeter followed his other teacher, Wieser's, bad example of practically never giving "chapter and verse" of his implicit quotations.

Reading Riedel, one quickly realizes that for Riedel, "speculation" is a much broader category than it is today: It comprises all economic decision-taking for the future. And in the thirty (!) odd pages that Riedel devotes to the entrepreneurial role in economics, *innovation* figures most prominently, while it is glossed over by most other German economic writing on the entrepreneur. So Riedel turns out to be the most immediate forerunner of Schumpeter in the German literature.

Riedel is old-fashioned as compared to the prevalent German protoneoclassical tradition of his time: he still takes labor to be productive only when it produces material goods, thus basically excluding the production of services from productive labor. But he neatly gets around this dilemma by distinguishing immediately and *intermediately* productive labor. Labor is manual labor and intellectual labor (*Körperarbeit und Geistesarbeit*) on the one hand and entrepreneurial labor and wage labor on the other. According to Riedel, then, the entrepreneur's contribution to social welfare is labor: but it is (intermediately) productive and (mainly) intellectual labor.[21]

Riedel enumerates five types of productive labor:[22] 1) *invention and discovery* (*Erfindung und Entdeckung*), 2) extraction (of raw materials), 3) manufacture, 4) productive modification (the German terms *Bereitung und Bearbeitung* cannot be easily rendered into English), and, finally, distribution (in the sense of transportation). Obviously, we shall focus on Riedel's first category: invention and discovery. He treats this

---

19. A. F. Riedel, *Nationalökonomie oder Volkswirthschaft*, 2 vol. (Berlin: F. H. Morin, 1838, 1839).

20. Menger, 230.

21. Riedel, *Nationalökonomie*, vol. 1, 127, § 167, 129, §169.

22. Ibid., 132 f. § 171.

extensively on six pages. And it should be noted that for Riedel, invention evidently is an *economic* judgment, not a mere technical process, such as innovation in Schumpeter's sense. Riedel wrote in 1838, long before Marx, who overstressed the purely technical side of material progress, so that only after 1867 Schumpeter's distinction between invention and innovation became important.

"The value of any commodity whatsoever"—Riedel explains—"presupposes the discovery of its usefulness." It was the biblical Adam who "made experiments and gathered experience and thus combined for the first time on earth nature and labour, a mainly intellectual (!) type of labour, for production."[23]

Riedel presents Adam, the biblical forefather of all mankind, as the obvious *pioneer* among all entrepreneurs. But innovation has not stopped with Adam and Eve. "Man still discovers in materials of known usefulness new characteristics which increase the degree of their utility. The intrinsic value of the soil, too, has only been researched in its smallest part and thus new discoveries and inventions still bring forth sizeable amounts of new material values."[24] "The discovery of new trade routes and markets (!) for home production, the invention of particular, more effective or cheaper sources of power for extraction, manufacture or transport and similar inventions directly generate a production of utility or value."[25] In "civilized societies," one can reckon with "continuous progress of inventions and discoveries."[26] Riedel even makes the point recently being stressed by Paul Romer.[27] "The peculiarity which distinguishes the production of inventions and discoveries from most other types of the application of productive labour consists in the fact that the production of an invention or discovery, once it has been achieved, cannot repeat itself continuously, but has happened once and for all."[28] In other words, innovation causes an extreme type of nonconvexity of the production set, economies of scale of a peculiar nature. Riedel, as is typical for the authors of German textbooks in the protoneoclassical tradition, treats the entrepreneur, as all other factors of production, twice in different parts of the book, once as factors and once as earners of income. In this second treatment he says:

---

23. Ibid., 133, § 172.
24. Ibid., 134, § 173.
25. Ibid., 135, § 174.
26. Ibid., 137, § 177.
27. Paul M. Romer, "Increasing Returns and Long-Run Growth," *Journal of Political Economy* 94(1986), 1002 ff.; "Endogenous Technological Change," *Journal of Political Economy* 98 (1990), 71 ff.
28. Riedel, *Nationalökonomie,* vol. 1, 1838, 136, § 176.

Of even greater importance is the labour of the entrepreneur in the field of speculation, where the demand resulting from human needs is observed in order to offer the consumers what they are lacking, where transport routes are searched out, where the best methods of production are scouted, where experiments with innovative ways of organizing an enterprise, with machines and tools are made, and where, driven by entrepreneurial ambition, all the entrepreneur's endeavours are directed towards a more advantageous use of the means of production which are combined in his enterprise in order to render him a higher profit.[29]

So we see that Riedel expounds in hardly less detail than Schumpeter *four* of the famous five types of innovation that the latter enumerates from the second edition of the *Theory of Economic Development* onward.[30] In particular, Riedel very explicitly deals with two of the types of innovation that are usually thought to be specifically Schumpeterian: the development of new trade routes and markets, on the one hand, and the exploitation of new raw materials, on the other. The emphasis on these types of innovation is no coincidence with Riedel: it has to do with his understanding of the fivefold nature of productive labor. Schumpeter differs from Riedel in two respects only. On the one hand, he explicitly distinguishes product innovation and process innovation. While Riedel, as the quotations show, does not at all limit himself to process innovations, the explicit distinction of Schumpeter is an obvious consequence of the consumer (or final demand) orientation of the Austrian School, which made product innovation appear as the very essence of all innovation. Secondly, Schumpeter adds a fifth category of innovation, namely the development of a strategic market position. In this, he stands alone. Among the orthodox German and Austrian economic theoreticians, only Schumpeter sees monopoly as largely beneficial to society.

Riedel, as I pointed out, though writing three quarter centuries before Schumpeter, was never forgotten in the Austrian School. I know, however, of no other similarly lengthy treatment of innovation in German or Austrian literature—and of no treatment so closely foreshadowing Schumpeter's thought. To write treatises on entrepreneurial profit was, on the other hand, common practice in Vienna before Schumpeter: As Menger was much interested in the entrepreneurial role,[31] this was to be expected. The habilitation theses of Gross and Mataja may be men-

---

29. Riedel, *Nationalökonomie*, vol. 2, 1839, 11, § 470.
30. Schumpeter, *Theorie der wirtschaftlichen Entwicklung*, 100 f.; *The Theory of Economic Development* (New York: OUP, 1961), 66.
31. Menger, *Grundsätze*, chap.3, 136 f., § 3 c.

tioned.[32] But they are curiously silent on innovation. I have repeatedly pointed out[33] that Schumpeter owes his heroic vision of the entrepreneur and the pertinent vocabulary to his teacher, Friedrich von Wieser. But here we may notice an innovation of Schumpeter's: while he focuses above all on the great entrepreneur, just as Wieser had done, Schumpeter is alone in stressing almost exclusively the great, the *epochal innovation*—while Riedel obviously had seen no need to distinguish great innovations from small. He suggests, rather, that all entrepreneurial activity, even the entrepreneur's humdrum day-to-day chores, are innovative. This is much closer to Hayek, especially in "Competition as a Discovery Procedure,"[34] where all entrepreneurial information gathering is basically innovative to such an extent that innovation in the narrower sense is not singled out.

As compared to Riedel, one more innovation of Schumpeter's with respect to innovation can be pointed out. Riedel summarizes: "Every innovative invention and discovery, which is made anywhere in the world, continuously mobilizes nearly everywhere new labourers or sets the old ones doubly in motion and thus excites all other productions to ever greater strength and variety."[35] In other words, innovation is wholly and solely beneficial. It is probably Schumpeter's most important contribution to stress creative *destruction,* the negative external effects or *business stealing,*[36] as well as the positive effects of economic growth and of the enhancement of welfare.

3

In the English classical tradition of economics, little attention is paid to credit, especially by the founders, Adam Smith and Ricardo. If credit is treated, it is examined solely as a substitute for money and with respect to its effect on the price level. John Stuart Mill's *Principles* does have a separate chapter, Book III, chapter 9, entitled "Of Credit, As a Substitute

---

32. Gustav Gross, *Die Lehre vom Unternehmergewinn* (Leipzig 1884); Viktor Mataja, *Der Unternehmergewinn. Ein Beitrag zur Lehre von der Güterveteilung in der Volkswirtschaft* (Vienna 1884).

33. Streissler, *Influence*; Erich Streissler, *"Arma virumque cano—Friedrich von Wieser, the Bard as Economist,"* in Die Wiener Schule der Nationalökonomie, Norbert Leser, ed. (Vienna, Cologne, Graz: Böhlau, 1986), 83 ff.

34. Friedrich August von Hayek, "Competition as a Discovery Procedure," in *New Studies in Philosophy, Politics, Economics and the History of Ideas,* ed. Friedrich A. von Hayek (London: Routledge, 1978), 179 ff.

35. Riedel, *Nationalökonomie,* 139, § 180.

36. See, e.g., Jean Tirole, *The Theory of Industrial Organization* (Cambridge, Mass. and London: MIT Press, 1988), 323 ff., 392 ff., 401 ff.

for Money(!)."³⁷ Here Mill in § 1 first points out that by "many people," the role of credit is much exaggerated into one of "national importance." The *real* effects of credit are discussed very briefly in § 2 of his chapter, where we are told that "though credit is but a transfer of capital from hand to hand, it is generally, and naturally, a transfer to hands more competent to employ the capital efficiently in production." And:

> While credit is thus indispensable for rendering the whole capital of the country productive, it is also a means by which the industrial talent of the country is turned to better account for purposes of production. Many a person who has either no capital of his own, or very little, but who has qualifications for business which are known and appreciated by some persons of capital, is enabled [by credit to employ] his industrial capacities [for] the increase of the public wealth.³⁸

After these very brief remarks, and without dwelling at all on the role of the banks in increasing productive efficiency through credit, Mill immediately turns to "a more intricate portion of the theory of credit . . . its influence on prices."³⁹

These "many people," who thought credit to be of "national importance," could, on the other hand, easily be found among German economists, French economists, and particularly Austrian economists. They thought it of paramount importance to create banks as instruments of industrial policy. And it is well known that the German, French, and Austrian banks (and later, of course, the Japanese banks modeled on them) were very active in the long-term financing of manufactuing enterprises, in contrast to the mere short-term financing of commercial business more typical of British or American banking. The eminent Austrian Schumpeterian (once Schumpeter's doctoral student), Eduard März, outlined the history of the Austrian *Credit-Anstalt* (modeled on the French "Credit Mobilier") as an industrial bank.⁴⁰ While the Austrian banks at first had been slow to start financing manufacturing firms, there was a veritable fever of *Gründungsgeschäfte,* literally "foundations of enterprises" through banks in Austria in Schumpeter's early youth, in

---

37. John Stuart Mill, *Principles of Political Economy with some of their Applications to Social Philosophy,* ed. Sir William Ashley (Fairfield: Augustus M. Kelley, [1848] 1976).
38. Mill, *Principles,* 512, 513, § 3.
39. Mill, *Principles,* 514, § 3.
40. Eduard März, *Österreichische Industrie- und Bankpolitik in der Zeit Franz Joseph I.* (Vienna: Europa Verlag, 1968).

the 1890s and the 1900s. I have pointed out elsewhere that Schumpeter probably misunderstood what actually happened then, being misled by the word *Gründungsgeschäfte*. For the banks hardly ever "founded" new industrial enterprises, as the word *Gründungsgeschäfte* would imply, but merely *incorporated already existing* and thriving unincorporated firms and introduced their stock on the stock exchange.[41]

But perhaps in his discussion of the relationship between credit and new entrepreneurial activity Schumpeter was not so much influenced by what was actually happening around him, but much rather by what the German language economists wrote, in other words not by empirical observation but by literary precepts. From Karl Heinrich Rau, the founder of the German textbook tradition, onward, the effect of credit is usually treated at length in the German textbooks.[42] The increase of the allocative efficiency of the use both of capital and of qualified managers is remarked upon, usually very much in the vein of John Stuart Mill quoted above—Rau's first edition antedating Mill by twenty-two years, of course. Rau already states that "The largest part of commercial enterprises are run with capital which the entrepreneurs have merely borrowed."[43] The old Austrian School was greatly interested in the role of credit—Albert Schäffle, Menger's predecessor, for example, writing on this topic. Friedrich von Wieser, one of Schumpeter's direct teachers, also treats credit thoroughly and extensively.[44]

In the nineteenth-century German language tradition of economics, the locus classicus on the role of credit is Carl Knies's monumental treatise *Geld und Credit* (Money and Credit), 1873 and 1879, the second book of which deals with credit.[45] Knies, though German, was closely linked to the Austrian School, for it was in Knies's seminar in Heidelberg that both Böhm-Bawerk and Wieser as young scholars had presented their first subjective value papers. And, lo and behold, in Knies we can find many of Schumpeter's specific notions on the relationship between credit and entrepreneurial activity, which were, in other words, quite familar in German economic thinking thirty years before Schumpeter started to publish.

Among the main assertions of Knies is the statement that as a rule,

---

41. Streissler, *Influence,* 74 ff.

42. See, e.g., Roscher, *Grundlagen,* book 1, chap. 6, altogether 13 pages in a textbook of some 570 pages. Rau, *Grundsätze,* has a somewhat shorter, but very substantial chapter on credit. See Rau III/14/3, 346 ff.

43. Rau, *Gundsätze,* 349, § 280.

44. Wieser, *Gesellschaftlichen Wirtschaft,* 169–78

45. Carl Knies, *Der Credit* (zweite Hälfte), 2.Abteilung von *Geld und Credit* (Berlin: Weidmann, 1879).

the entrepreneur is *different* in person from the capitalist and that the *distinctive class of entrepreneurs has been created by the credit market:* "The credit market makes possible the division of the persons of the *asset owner* and of the *principal of the enterprise.* The *operation* as such of an enterprise can be made a particular calling . . . the class of entrepreneurs arises next to that of the rentiers."[46] And not only that: entrepreneurs without capital are typically of greater ability than entrepreneurs who own their capital. In particular, the greater entrepreneurs will normally work exclusively with other people's capital. And these "greater entrepreneurs," who depend on credit, are characterized by Knies with the very words that Schumpeter would use for the creative entrepreneur: "active energy in their work, a gift for organizing, the ability to command, perspicacity, a quick and steady will, anticipation of future events, combination of dispersed particulars, and the like regularly turn them into men who are typically also politically (!) important."[47] Knies summarizes that credit makes it possible to enlarge the scale—or the number (the language here is ambiguous)—of enterprises as far as possible, in particular in times of rising prices.

A further peculiarity in Schumpeter's *Theory of Economic Development* can be traced to Knies. It is curious that Schumpeter should make so much of the importance of credit for founding enterprises, when actually before and immediately after the First World War in many cases German and Austrian firms were established by floating common stock on the stock market. Knies, however, considers the *stockholder* in a widely held corporation as *practically indistinguishable from a mere creditor!* He lumps stock holders, bond holders, and other creditors together under the portmanteau caption "credit." The banks have created "a class of creditors(!) : the money capitalists," who deal on the stock exchanges.[48] In other words, the idea that the average stock holder is at the mercy of the manager-entrepreneur, which Schumpeter voices in *Capitalism, Socialism, and Democracy,*[49] is already implicitly suggested in Knies.

---

46. Knies, *Der Credit,* 187: "Der Creditverkehr ermöglicht die Trennung der Person des *Vermögensbesitzers* und der des *Geschäftsinhabers.* Der Geschäft*betrieb* als solcher . . . kann zu einem besonderen Lebensberufe . . . gemacht werden . . . neben den Stand der *Rentner* tritt der Stand der *Unternehmer.*"
47. Knies, *Der Credit,* 187 f.: 'Eine rührige Arbeitsenergie, Organisationstalent, Befähigung zum 'Commandiren,' Schaftsicht, rascher schwankenfreier Wille, Voraussicht von Kommendem, Combination von verstreutem Enzelnen u. dgl. machen sie zu regelmäßig auch politisch bedeutsamen Männern."
48. Knies, *Der credit,* 199.
49. Joseph A. Schumpeter, *Capitalism, Socialism and Democracy* (New York: Harper, 1942).

In what way was Schumpeter's treatment of the role of credit in stimulating entrepreneurship innovative? While Riedel had discussed innovation at length as one (though not the only) important function of the entrepreneur, Knies had not suggested that credit, which creates the modern entrepreneur, also creates the innovator. Furthermore credit, according to Knies, creates a *social class* of entrepreneurs, not so much the heroic *individuals* of Schumpeter; though Knies then characterizes the "greater entrepreneurs" as a class of leaders, even in political life. So Schumpeter is more individualistic in his treatment of the personality of the entrepreneur.[50] In this, however, he only echoes Roscher, who likens entrepreneurs to the great military leaders of history, like Wallenstein,[51] and, in particular, he echoes the heroic "Führer" vocabulary of his own teacher, Wieser.[52]

4

Schumpeter has often been quoted as the most important author to assign a positive economic role to monopolies, seeing them in a much more favorable light than was usual among economists in general. Schumpeter held that monopolies are quite often favorable to technical progress and, thus, could eventually turn into cheaper sources of supply for consumers than the perfectly competitive enterprises of the text-book, which (for lack of profit) are unable to invest in innovation.[53] In this respect he was actually much more innovative than in his analysis of the innovative entrepreneur proper. I have not been able to find any significant predecessors of this line of Schumpeter's thought in the general orthodox German or Austrian economic literature in the century before the publication of his seminal *Theory of Economic Development*.

However, the twenty years before the publication of this book had actually witnessed a great wave of cartelization and monopolization in German and Austrian—and, of course, also in American—industry. The Austrian banks that had "founded" many new industrial enterprises in this period (i.e., actually had turned existing firms into joint stock companies) and that tried to sell the shares to the public, only to discover that often they could not sell as much as they hoped so that they

---

50. In his highly perceptive "commentary" Kiichiro Yagi rightly remarks that Schumpeter's interest in the heroic entrepreneur as an individual need not imply, however, individualism in the sense of methodological individualism.

51. Roscher, *Die Grundlagen der Nationalökonomie,* 402, § 195.

52. See, e.g., Wieser, *Arma Virumque Cano;* see further examples quoted in Streissler, "Arma Virumque Cano."

53. Schumpeter, *Wirtschaftlichen Entwicklung,* 112 f.

were saddled with increasing portfolios of industrial stock—these Austrian banks did everything in their power to *suppress* competition between the firms affliated with them. To this end, the large Austrian banks founded the *Kontrollbank* as their joint instrument of industrial control, whose main duty it was to see to it that firms largely belonging to one bank did not compete—in the sense of cutting price—with firms belonging to the same or even to other banks.[54] "Credit," thus, created monopoly power! Another popular notion in Germany around the turn of the century was that German firms should not compete against each other in foreign markets. Export cartels were seen as an effective means of insuring maximum returns from international trade in the national interest.

German or Austrian economists of the Younger Historical School were far less critical of monopolies than the classical or "neoclassical" English economists; and it should be remembered that Schumpeter, very early in his academic career, and even before he came in contact with the leaders of the Austrian School in Vienna, Wieser and Böhm-Bawerk, studied with exponents of this school in Vienna, with Juraschek and Inama-Sternegg; and that he later wrote a very appreciative article on the leader of the Younger Historical School, Gustav von Schmoller of Berlin.[55] It has been remarked that, in spite of their socially reformist veneer, the members of the Younger Historical School were, on the whole, rather conservative: they described what they found, and tended to assume that what existed was good.[56] This was true for monopoly. Kleinwächter, an Austrian economist, had already published a treatise on cartels in 1883.[57] And the locus classicus of the German-language literature on cartels and trusts in the most impressive early years of Schumpeter's youth was the widely read and frequently reprinted book by Robert Liefmann of Freiburg in Germany, *Kartelle und Trusts,* first published in 1905. Some of Schumpeter's ideas can be found there.

Liefmann regards cartels, in general, in a quite favorable light and collects an armory of arguments in their favor, though not always informed by sound theory (e.g., he does not seem really to understand a demand curve): cartels reduce the risk of using capital and adjust

---

54. See März, *Österreichische Industrie,* 370 f.

55. See Schumpeter, *"Gustav von Schmoller."*

56. That the German Younger Historical School was actually highly conservative is one of the main tenets of Menger's last student in the "habilitation," Richard Schüller. See Richard Schüller, *Die Wirtschaftspolitik der Historischen Schule* (Berlin: Heymanns, 1899). See also Streissler, *"Carl Menger,"* 185.

57. Friedrich von Kleinwächter, *Die Kartelle. Ein Beitrag zur Organisation der Volkswirtschaft* (Innsbruck: 1883).

production better to demand;[58] they *increase* production and the number of firms in an industry in general in spite of their attempt to keep the price high (an argument that could be correct with a falling marginal cost curve, but with no ability to recover the fixed cost of additional investment in the case of marginal cost pricing by competitive firms);[59] they increase wages and at the same time increase job security;[60] they offer consumers a smoother supply (an argument that is contradicted two pages later, where Liefmann says that, in a downswing, cartels adjust their production downward and keep prices constant, while competitors do the opposite).[61] A decrease in the variability of price due to cartels improves the precision of calculation of wholesale and retail traders.[62] Most interestingly, Liefmann introduces a variant of Schumpeter's subsequent argument of the "low price" monopolist (in the long run) when he points out that while cartels will charge higher prices than competitors in a recession, they are unable to charge high prices in periods of good demand, because this would immediately attract price-cutting new enterprises:[63] In effect, he suggests a *contestable market* argument.[64] Liefmann's long-run conclusion is this: "Experience has in any case shown that all cartels which exist for any length of time cause a very substantial increase in production and supply; and if this is not due to the incentive offered for the foundation of new enterprises it is due to the increase of the scale of production of cartel members."[65] The fact that in foreign markets they frequently sell below their home market price is no loss to the home country, but serves to stabilize production and employment at home.[66]

Liefmann comes closest to the spirit of Schumpeter in a six- to seven-page chapter on the effect of cartels on *technical progress* or innovation. He explicitly rejects the argument that cartels tend to stick to and thus preserve existing technologies; in fact, competition remains strong enough within them so that they eagerly seek out new methods of production (an argument that could easily be extended to single firm

---

58. Robert Liefmann, *Kartelle und Trusts und die Weiterbildung der volkswirtschaft-lichen Organisation* (Stuttgart: E.H.Moritz, [1905] 1920), 53 f.
59. Ibid., 64.
60. Ibid., 82 ff.
61. Ibid., 97.
62. Ibid., 99.
63. Ibid., 100 ff.
64. See, e.g., William J. Baumol, "Contestable Markets: An Uprising in the Theory of Industry Structure," *American Economic Review* 72 (1982): 1 ff.
65. Liefmann, *Kartelle und Trusts,* 101.
66. Liefmann, *Kartelle und Trusts,* 116.

monopolies if they are threatened by entry). "So far no cases are known where cartels have suppressed the application of important technical improvements." In fact, they can improve the spread of innovation by making it available to all cartel members. Frequently they will create *new firms* (or merely new plants; the terminology is ambiguous here) in order to put the new techniques into practice.[67]

So we see that Schumpeter only had to pick up the arguments for the economic advantages of monopolies that the German-language historical literature of his time held ready for him. Even the argument that monopolies advance innovation was "prefabricated." Being much the better theoretician, he could simply improve on these ideas in obvious ways (or at least in ways that seem obvious today).

In this he was marching in the same direction as his immediate teacher, Friedrich von Wieser, who dealt at length with monopolies in his textbook, *The Theory of Social Economics,* published in 1914, slightly after Schumpeter's *Theory of Economic Development,* but of whose arguments Schumpeter must have learned previously from the lectures he attended.[68] Wieser, who admired anything big, thought the classical criticism of monopolies as welfare-reducing was outdated and no longer applicable.[69] He explicitly says that because of the benefits of vertical integration, large-scale "trusts" will produce at (much) lower cost than small-scale competitors, and he concludes that they might even have price lowering effects by throwing the most inefficient competitors out of the market and then selling at the marginal cost price of the remaining competitors.[70] Large-scale integrated enterprises with monopoly power he regards as the hotbed of technical progress and the breeding ground as well as the instrument of "selection" of entrepreneurial "leaders."[71] "The rise of these great personalities and leaders is, however, accompanied by the fall of many other entrepreneurs,"[72] explains Wieser, thus even suggesting the idea of "creative destruction" for the case of trusts. Obviously these were notions that Schumpeter had only to elaborate.

5

While the general orthodox German-language economic theory had little to say on the positive side of monopolies and their connection with techni-

---

67. Ibid., 90 ff., 92, 95.
68. Wieser, *Theorie der gesellschaftlichen Wirtschaft,* 151–62.
69. Ibid., 155.
70. Ibid., 161.
71. Ibid., 162.
72. Ibid., 162 (my translation, as I do not have the English edition available).

cal progress, Schumpeter, with his truly Catholic appreciation of a wide range of methodological positions in economics, could thus find inspiration in the contemporary treatises of the Younger Historical School and that of his teacher, Wieser, the member of the Austrian School closest to historicism. But he could also find like inspiration in Karl Marx and the German-language Marxist literature of his day. As is well known, and as he himself frequently pointed out, among orthodox economists, Schumpeter is one of those most strongly influenced by Marxism.

Das Kapital, by Karl Marx, itself, assigns, of course, a very active role to the capitalist, especially the role of creating technical progress. The first volume of this tome, the one actually completed and published by Marx, has a three-page analysis of all the effects of the creation of an innovation and of the process of diffusion of such an innovation throughout an industry. The analysis is very close to Schumpeter's "creative destruction."[73] (That Marx should show a total lack of understanding of the underlying demand curve is beside the point here.)

But it is above all *Das Finanzkapital,* of Rudolf Hilferding, published in 1910, but, according to the preface written in substantial parts in 1905, that obviously influenced Schumpeter strongly.[74] Hilferding, born in 1877, was Schumpeter's five-and-a-half-years-older Viennese compatriot; and they both attended—together with Mises, Otto Bauer, and Emil Lederer—Böhm-Bawerk's famous seminar in 1905–1906, when *Das Finanzkapital* was already completed in its main parts. The evident strong influence of Hilferding on the Austrian School in the second decade of the twentieth century can be noticed far and wide: on Mises, on the old Wieser, in his *Theorie der Gesellschaftlichen Wirtschaft* of 1914, and so on; certainly not only on Schumpeter.

But of all of the Austrians, it is Schumpeter who follows Hilferding most closely. Hilferding's main theme is the connection between the development of large-scale industry and bank credit on the one hand, and of bank credit and monopolization on the other. The preface already says:

> The characteristic features of "modern" capitalism are the processes of concentration, which appear on the one hand as the "elimination of free competition" due to the formation of cartels and trusts, on the other hand as the ever closer connection between the capital of the banks and industrial capital . . . capital . . . takes on

---

73. Karl Marx, *Das Kapital. Kritik der politischen Oekonomie.* Vol. 1, MEGA 23 (Berlin: Dietz, [1867] 1969), chap. 10, p. 335 ff.

74. Rudolf Hilferding, *Das Finanzkapital. Eine Studie über die jüngste Entwicklung des Kapitalismus* (Frankfurt, Vienna: Europa Verlag, [1910] 1968).

the form of financial capital [*Finanzkapital*] which is its highest and most abstract manifestation.[75]

The typical (continental, in contrast to English) "modern" development, according to Hilferding, is that banks finance fixed industrial capital. Credit develops from that for mere payment purposes to "capital credit." The use of such credit becomes a competitive necessity for industry. But, at the same time, industrial firms fall under the control of banks; and this reinforces all latent tendencies toward industrial concentration. Industrial organization is changed and the firms are transformed into joint stock companies.[76]

Above, I criticized Schumpeter because he speaks of the central role of bank credit for the foundation of new enterprises, while in his time these were much rather financed by placing common stock on the capital market and, actually, often were not even newly founded, but just reorganized as legal entitities in the form of joint stock companies. This position of Schumpeter's is easily explained when we see that it is derived from Hilferding: for Hilferding, continuing the line suggested by Knies, explicitly considers common stock as a form of credit created by the banks,[77] as the common stock holder acquires a highly liquid financial title and has as tenuous a connection with the actual running of the enterprise as a creditor. In fact, Hilferding, soon to be followed in this respect by Wieser,[78] is one of the first important economic authors to stress pure managerial (and banking) control of the widely held joint stock company,[79] a position later championed by Schumpeter,[80] who did not have to learn about it from the American authors of the thirties,[81] as this position was already a

---

75. Hilferding, *Das Finanzkapital*, 17: "Das Charakteristische des 'modernen' Kapitalismus bilden aber jene Konzentrationsvorgänge, die einerseits in der 'Aufhebung der freien Konkurrenz' durch Bildung von Kartellen und Trusts, andrerseits in der immer innigeren Beziehung zwischen Bankkapital und industriellem Kapital erscheinen . . . das Kapital . . . (nimmt) die Form des Finanzkapitals an, die seine höchste und abstrakteste Erscheinungsform ist." (As I do not have an English edition of *Das Finanzkapital* available, the translation is my own.)

76. Ibid., 113, 115, 116, 118, 123, 136.

77. Ibid., 140.

78. Wieser, *Theorie der gesellschaftlichen wirtschaft*, 228 ff., § 63. Wieser analyzes what he calls the *Beamtenunternehmung,* the "civil service type" enterprise, governed by educated managers. He says (p. 231) that the large scale enterprise has "decomposed" or "dissolved" (*zersetzt*) the role of the owners of capital.

79. Hilferding, *Das Finanzkapital*, 169.

80. E.g., Schumpeter, *Capitalism, Socialism and Democracy*, Part II, chap. 12, sec. 3.

81. E.g., Adolph A. Berle, Jr. and Gardiner C. Means, *The Modern Corporation and Private Property* (New York: Macmillan, 1932); Schumpeter, *Capitalism, Socialism and Democracy,* does *not* quote this influential text.

widely held one in his Austrian youth. Furthermore, Hilferding analyzes extensively the *Gründungsgeschäft* (literally, the business of founding new enterprises) by the banks, including the profits made that way, and is quite explicit in stating that the firms in question are frequently not "founded" in the literal sense, but just reorganized and introduced on the stock exchange.[82] In his further discussion, Hilferding does not distinguish sharply between newly founded productive enterprises and merely reorganized ones, but lumps these processes together. This is quite logical in the case of Hilferding, who sees an enterprise solely as a system of decisions and control. Incorporating an enterprise that was previously run by individual persons as a joint stock company in this sense actually amounts to the "foundation" of a "new" decision-making unit. Lumping together foundation and mere reorganization is, however, no longer logical in the case of Schumpeter, where the enterprise is a system of production and of consumer relationships; these frequently do not change when the legal form of the enterprise is changed by incorporation, so that in Schumpeter's sense, no new enterprise would be founded.

One of Hilferding's main themes is the *close connection between bank credit* (in his wide sense) *and the tendencies toward monopoly*. The banks strive to eliminate competition. "Industrial capital owes it to the support of bank capital if the elimination of competition takes place already in a phase of economic development where, without the help of the banks, free competition would still persist."[83] Capitalist industry stimulates concentration in banking; for it needs large banks. But a concentrated banking system in its turn stimulates industrial concentration and creates cartels and trusts.[84] "Financial capital reaches its apogee in monopolizing industry."[85] Hilferding is the first major author to announce "monopoly capitalism" (though without using this term) as the supreme and final stage of capitalism and also a product of economic "necessity." To him it is already—as both orderly and anti-individualist—a kind of socialism and, thus, the final stage of capitalism before the "real" socialism.[86] Monopoly is not at all bad, but rather "good" in the sense of creating much more efficient production, and especially as eliminating "useless" wholesale and retail trade.[87] Monopolies will sometimes charge lower prices to consumers; and if there remains any outside or even latent com-

82. Hilferding, *Das Finanzkapital*, 171.
83. Hilferding, *Das Finanzkapital*, 257.
84. Ibid., 306.
85. Ibid., 309.
86. Ibid., 244, 303, 333.
87. Ibid., 294 f., 301 f.

petition, they are forced to introduce new technologies.[88] Points already made in part by Knies and Liefmann are, thus, reiterated by Hilferding in a way very close to what Schumpeter wrote. Many of Schumpeter's positions are foreshadowed in Hilferding. It is true that Hilferding does not know the creative entrepreneur. But, with him, monopolies created by bank credit head the march of progress. This anonymous and collective movement then becomes personalized and individualistic in Schumpeter.

6

Schumpeter is one of the first authors to divide economic theory into a *static* and a *dynamic* part; and for him the theory of the entrepreneur is the centerpiece of dynamic analysis. He discusses this division at length already in his very first book, *Das Wesen und der Hauptinhalt der theoretischen Nationalökonomie*, 1908.[89] There he says that he is only adopting a terminology "recently" come into use, though he does not consider it a happy one:[90] Evidently Schumpeter (who, as usual, does not quote) can only be following J. B. Clark, who had used this distinction in *The Distribution of Wealth*, 1899, [91] a book that Schumpeter had reviewed in great detail in one of his very first articles, already in the year 1906.[92] Static theory, for Schumpeter, is the theory at a point of time, for given circumstances, and under unchanging conditions, static theory being with him largely equivalent with equilibrium analysis,[93] while dynamic theory concerns itself with "phenomena of development," with "the great tendencies of development," with "large changes"; in other words, from the start with that kind of development Haberler in his obituary called the "grandeur of the . . . system."[94] What phenomena, Schumpeter asks, can be analyzed only in such a "dynamic" framework? He thinks himself on uncontroversial ground when he assigns the analysis of profit to "dynamic" situations.[95] And, indeed, we saw that, at the very start of German economic reasoning on entrepreneurial profit, Hufeland had regarded such profit as a disequi-

---

88. Ibid., 318 f.

89. Joseph Schumpeter, *Das Wesen und der Hauptinhalt der theoretischen Nationalökonomie* (Berlin: Duncker und Humblot, [1908] 1970), 176 ff., 614–26.

90. Ibid., 182.

91. John Bates Clark, *The Distribution of Wealth. A Theory of Wages, Interest and Profits* (New York: Macmillan, 1899). For "statics" and "dynamics," see 30 ff.

92. Joseph Schumpeter, "Professor Clarks Verteilungstheorie," *Zeitschrift für Volkswirtschaft, Sozialpolitik und Verwaltung* 15 (1906): 325–33.

93. Schumpeter, 1908, *Der theoretischen Nationalökonomie* 28, 176 ff.

94. Ibid., 186, 518, 618. See, furthermore, Haberler, *"Schumpeter,"* 363.

95. Schumpeter, *Der theoretischen Nationalökonomie*, 431.

librium phenomenon.[96] That the theory of economic "crisis," as Schumpeter calls it, has to be dynamic[97] is certainly also uncontroversial. Not many of the mainstream German economists, though, would have agreed with Schumpeter that no entrepreneurial *activity* "in the true sense" can take place under static conditions.[98] Truly innovative, however, is Schumpeter's assignment of saving, but also of credit, and in particular of the rate of interest, to the category of economic phenomena analyzable not in static terms, but only in a dynamic framework.[99] Later, when he became more explicit on the latter point, asserting that there cannot be a rate of interest in a stationary state, he was to clash violently, as is well known, with Böhm-Bawerk.[100] In his first book, Schumpeter already announces his methodological program: "Economic history and economic description should be consulted nearly exclusively in the case of dynamics—and not least those of *German* provenance."[101] We have seen that Schumpeter later actually followed this precept, adding the analysis of the effects of monopoly to "dynamic" analysis (in his sense) for good measure.

His teacher, Friedrich von Wieser, used a quite different—and rather woolly—concept of economic "statics" and of economic equilibrium and does not use the category "dynamic analysis" at all.[102] But, terminology apart, the idea of assigning the main "dynamic" role (i.e., the main role in economic development) to the entrepreneur is evidently taken over and adapted for Schumpeter's purposes from the philosophy of history of Wieser. In his partly autobiographic essay, *Arma virumque cano,*[103] of 1907, Wieser develops a framework of thought in which mass phenomena are contrasted with what he calls "the Great-Man-Theory." Mass phenomena, he suggests, properly are the field of the social sciences. In this he follows an inspiration that he traces, rather curiously and autobiographically, to Herbert Spencer.[104] These mass phenomena consti-

---

96. See Hufeland, *Neue Grundlegung,* and the ideas stressed in the text.

97. Schumpeter, *Der theoretischen Nationalökonomie,* 615.

98. Ibid., 433.

99. Ibid., 184, 619, 390–430.

100. See Eugen Böhm von Bawerk, "Eine 'dynamische' Theorie des Kapitalzinses," *Zeitschrift für Volkswirtschaft, Sozialpolitik und Verwaltung* 22 (1913); no less than 65 pages! [Reprint: Böhm-Bawerk, *Kleinere Abhandlungen,* Franz X. Weiss, ed., vol. 2 (Vienna, Leipzig: Hölder-Pichler-Tempsky, 1926), 520–85]; Joseph A. Schumpeter, "Eine 'dynamische' Theorie des Kapitalzinses. Eine Entgegnung," *Zeitschrift für Volkswirtschaft, Sozialpolitik und Verwaltung* 22 (1913): 599 ff., a response of 40 (!) pages; and then a further reply by Böhm-Bawerk.

101. Schumpeter, *Der theoretischen Nationalökonomie,* 617.

102. Wieser, *Theorie der gesellschaftlichen Wirtschaft,* 40.

103. Wieser, *Arma Virumque Caro.* See also Streissler, *Influence.*

104. Wieser, *Arma Virumque Caro,* 4.

tute "nameless history."[105] The necessarily epic story of the "great men" is properly the field of *history* in the narrower sense. And it is these great men who create all that is new, all development, "the real innovations":

> Again and again out of the free realm of the spirit the spark of talent, of genius lights up, unexpectedly and surprisingly, in order to open up ever wider the paths of development. . . . Without the great men there would be no development, they give the incentives by which humanity grows. . . . The progress to which they point is only fully reached when their example is imitated by the others.[106]

"Only those innovations persist which pass the test of common fulfill-ment. . . . The personality of the leaders . . . remains . . . always of importance; it even grows in importance with the tasks of civilization. No progress can be accomplished without leadership, not in war and especially not in peace." "The innovator steps on virgin soil."[107]

Schumpeter's "creative entrepreneur" is evidently a subspecies of his teacher's idea of the "great man" in history. In his economic text, Wieser uses somewhat more restrained language, but Schumpeter's entire termi-nology is already there in Wieser's *Theorie der gesellschaftlichen Wirtschaft:*

> It is not capital which brings success, for capital itself is largely formed out of accrued profits. It is its role as market leader which has brought success to an enterprise. The men who pioneered new ways had to be supremely gifted men who combined technical abili-ties, a sense for the market and organizational power and in addi-tion the audacity of the innovator.

> In the capitalist enterprise the greatest entrepreneurial personalities have grown to their fullest stature, the audacious technical innova-tors, the organizers knowledgable of human nature, the farsighted bankers, the reckless speculators, the leaders of the trusts who conquer the world.[108]

I have pointed out elsewhere to what extent Friedrich von Wieser dif-fered in his ideas on entrepreneurial activity from Schumpeter.[109] But the family likeness is obvious.

---

105. Ibid., 6.
106. Ibid., 8.
107. Ibid., 9, 10.
108. Wieser, *Theorie der gesellschaftlichen Wirtschaft*, 252, 231. My translations.
109. Streissler, *Influence*, 93 ff.

7

To us today, Schumpeter seems a very different type of economist from those representative of the traditions of economic thought that most of us know best—very different, say, from Léon Walras, or Alfred Marshall, or Keynes, or Samuelson, or Arrow, or even Milton Friedman. In his time, and in the German-language tradition of economics, however, Schumpeter evidently fits in very well: He is innovative, but not totally different. In fact, he may be regarded as a relic of German economic thought: He took up ideas from different corners within the framework of German-language social sciences and from different time periods and welded them together into a much more appealing whole.

But is he also an Austrian of the Austrian School? The modern representatives of the Neo-Austrian School in the United States and Great Britain do not seem to think so. In his early work before the First World War, Schumpeter had, of course, written copiously on the subjective value topics of the Austrians. But his writing on these topics has not stood the test of history particularly well. He himself thought these topics to be of a "static" nature; and economic "statics," to him, appeared to be of less importance than the development of a "dynamic" *Theory of Economic Development,* particularly as the "static" theory of his day was already highly developed in the Austrian tradition. The history of thought has proved him to be right, at least with regard to his own contributions to static economics, now only little known.

Nevertheless, Schumpeter was an Austrian economist, with the usual pronounced streak of subjectivism. He was un-Austrian, it is true, in his use of many ideas from the Younger German Historical School and from Marxism. But he turned these "objective hsitorical phenomena" into a much more personalized form, giving them a much more individualistic and "idealistic" treatment. His individualism was, it is true, the heroic individualism of Friedrich von Wieser, rather than the subjectivism and individualism of Menger's common man. Such heroic individualism unfortunately may entail fascist leanings, as we can see by studying Friedrich von Wieser in his old age.[110] Schumpeter, it is true, was not a fervent classical liberal in his value judgments, as were Menger, or Böhm-Bawerk, or Mises, or Hayek. But not all members of the Austrian School in its Austrian heyday—stretching over three quarters of a century—were pure and unadulterated classical liberals. Nor did Schumpeter think in terms of the systemic framework of Adam

---

110. See Friedrich Wieser, *Das Gesetz der Macht* (Vienna: Springer, 1926). On the fascist leanings of Wieser in his old age, see Streissler, *Influence,* 86 ff.

Smith,of whom, in fact, he thought little.[111] But should we exclude Schumpeter from the Austrian School merely on these grounds? If the Neo-Austrian School thinks of "Austrianism" as a contrast program to the run of the mill neoclassicism (to "statics," as Schumpeter would have said), is not Schumpeter the perfect example of an Austrian who tried to go beyond the traditions of Marshall and Walras? For, much as he admired the two, he actually did not follow them in the least. And if "process analysis" is to the Neo-Austrians the very essence of Austrianism,[112] is not Schumpeter second to none in his attempt to sketch a process analysis of economic development? Furthermore, it was Schumpeter who, in his thesis of "habilitation" of 1908, first coined and systematically discussed the phrase "methodological individualism,"[113] a concept that he explicitly espoused.

So he is a thoroughly "Austrian" economist in part of his work, strongly influenced, as all the Austrians were, by the older "protoneoclassical" tradition of German economics from before the time of the Austrian School. For an "Austrian" economist, however, Schumpeter also saw an unusual amount of merit in the traditions of the German Younger Historical School, and the more so the longer he lived. His *Business Cycles* may, in fact, be considered the last (and one of the most important) monographs of the Younger German Historical School.[114] Above, I have sketched his methodological position, quoting already from his very first book: "Economic history and economic description should be consulted nearly exclusively in the case of dynamics." So the more he turned to "economic dynamics" (in his sense) as his main task in life, the more he tended to become historical, and the more he tended to

---

111. Joseph A. Schumpeter, *History of Economic Analysis,* ed. E. B. Schumpeter (London: OUP, 1954), 181–94. Schumpeter makes the harsh judgement: "the *Wealth of Nations* contained no really novel ideas" (p. 185). Another statement tells us perhaps more about Schumpeter than Smith: Schumpeter charges Smith with a lack of "understanding of human nature" as "no woman, excepting his mother, ever played a role in his existence" (p. 182).

112. Haberler, *Joseph Alois Schumpeter,* says of his time: "Schumpeter is usually regarded as a member of the Austrian school" (p. 342), but classifies him rather "as a scholar . . . a citizen of the world" (p. 342). Still, he thinks "his theory of cost may be termed 'Austrian' " (p. 343). For the process analytic approach, "markets as processes," championed especially by Kirzner, see, e.g., Israel M. Kirzner, "Austrian School of Economics," in *The New Palgrave, A Dictionary of Economics,* ed. John Eatwell et.al., Vol.1, A to D (London: Macmillan, 1987), 145 ff., especially 149; also *Method, Process, and Austrian Economics, Essays in Honor of Ludwig von Mises,* ed. Israel M. Kirzner (Lexington Free Press, 1982).

113. Swedberg, *Joseph A. Schumpeter,* 26.

114. Joseph A. Schumpeter, *Business Cycles. A Theoretical, Historical, and Statistical Analysis of the Capitalist Process* (New York and London: McGraw Hill, 1939).

become descriptive. As is well known, Carl Menger, in the "First Methodenstreit," clashed with the Younger German Historical School and its leader, Gustav von Schmoller; and his school followed him in this. But the conflict had abated by around 1910. After all, Menger had never denied the justification for historical and quantitative research, and the historicists had not attacked theoretical concepts per se as long as they were validated empirically. The actual methodological conflict was rather esoteric: On the one hand, it concerned the basically ideological question of the proper understanding of, and therefore the role for, the state and, on the other, it served as a labeling device as to who was to be considered a proper candidate for professorial chairs of economics in specific (German-speaking) areas. Neither question interested Schumpeter. So he grasped at the olive branch proffered by Max Weber, an economist and sociologist equally highly regarded both in Germany and in Austria: There was to be a "Social Economics," something in between historical and purely theoretical economics. Schumpeter espoused this concept and made it his own, and in this respect became more of a traditional "German" than an "Austrian" economist. On the other hand, he remained completely "Austrian" in his thorough theoretical grounding.[115] Here, again, Max Weber provided a bridge to German thought on the social sciences in Schumpeter's day: For with Max Weber, Schumpeter thought "that theoretical economics should not take a political stance,"[116] so that a theoretical position helped to separate economics from the all too prevalent value judgments of German interwar economics. It is true that, at least before the First World War, few Austrian economists worked empirically. But they did not consider empirical work illegitimate. Schumpeter, the cofounder of the Econometric Society, in this respect belongs more to the German historical tradition than to the Austrian. Thus, in Schumpeter, influences of the Austrian School and of the Younger German Historical School mingled in a unique way. But it is important to remember that it was, above all, German and Austrian thought that shaped him, and important to remember that many of his ideas were easily recognizable in his home countries, that they were, in fact, apart from important variations, quite common in the German-speaking academy.

---

115. Swedburg, *Joseph A. Schumpeter,* 70, quotes the well-known German economist—and habilitation pupil of Schumpeter—Erich Schneider: "The assumption of teaching by Schumpeter in Bonn was a sensation for the academic world of economics. For the first time since decades, theory was taught again at a German university."

116. Swedberg, *Joseph A. Schumpeter,* 25.

Commentary

Kiichiro Yagi

In his essay a decade ago (Streissler 1981) Professor Streissler presented a vivid picture of the young Schumpeter. According to him, the young Schumpeter intentionally challenged customary views of the old Viennese society, but even so, still retained several typically Viennese conceptions in his views of banks and credit.

Now he invites us to consider German and Austrian literature, in which he finds the roots of Schumpeter's roots. I cannot but admire his thorough research, which recalls to mind such almost-forgotten names as those of Gottlieb Hufeland, Karl Heinrich Rau, and A. F. Riedel. These early nineteenth-century theorists were the precursors of Schumpeter's ideas of the entrepreneur and innovation!

Professor Streissler has found the very Schumpeterian relationship between bank credit and enterpreneurial activity, as well as the advantage of monopolies, in the literature of the German Historical School and of Austrian Marxism. But he also maintains that Schumpeter was still an Austrian in his subjectivism and in his stress on process analysis.

For Schumpeter, however, credit, innovation, entrepreneur, profit from disequilibrium, and so on, were elements of "a distinct capitalist process." Following the preface to the English edition of *The Theory of Economic Development* (Schumpeter 1980, xi), Schumpeter began his work on the theory of interest and the theory of the business cycle side by side. Because Böhm-Bawerk had been his teacher, I assume that the study of interest theory was undertaken as an academic task. Schumpeter's admiration of Léon Walras's theory grew out of this academic interest.

But in the other case, business cycle theory, Schumpeter was guided by contemporary literature of the Historical School, as well as of Marxism. Werner Sombart (1904) suggested that the study of the crises must be transformed into the study of the business cycle. In Vienna, near Schumpeter, Inama-Sternegg's statistics seminar discussed Clément Juglar's cycle theory (Somary 1955, 33f.), and Otto Bauer published his notes on

Marx's crisis theory (Bauer 1904). I think that Schumpeter's interest in the dynamics of the capitalist economy can be properly understood in this move to the crisis/cycle theory.

Since Bauer could not devote enough time to economics, it was Rudolf Hilferding, instead, who seems to have encouraged Schumpeter through a footnote in his *Finanzkapital:* "It is perfectly consistent for Schumpeter to reduce economics to a statics in order to keep the marginal utility theory intact. However it must ultimately be a dynamics, i.e., the theory of the laws of motion of capitalist society" (Hilferding 1910, 103).

Professor Streissler points out that Schumpeter was inclined to stress the role of bank credit in founding new business enterprises, rather than issuing shares and bonds. From what did this bias arise? Could Schumpeter provide a frame fit to analyze the financial market? I suspect that, in his view, the introduction of investors might imperil the Schumpeterian heroic vision of the entrepreneur.

Last but not least, the remark that Schumpeter's view of the entrepreneur is more individualistic than that of Karl Knies or Hilferding caught my attention. But I would like to ask what kind of individualism he applied in his analysis of dynamics. Enthusiasm, leadership, and imitation? These are just the opposite of what one associates with the term *methodological individualism.*

Was Schumpeter an individualist or a subjectivist? By replacing "Schumpeter" with "Schumpeterians," I would like to pose this question to the economists of the International J. A. Schumpeter Society.

REFERENCES

Bauer, Otto. 1904. "Marx' Theorie der Wirtschaftskrisen." *Neue Zeit* 23, no. 1 (5): 133–38, (6): 164–70.
Hilferding, Rudolf. 1910. *Das Finanzkapital. Marx-Studien* 3. Vienna: I. Brand.
Juglar, Clément. 1862. *Des crises commerciales et de leur retour périodique en France, en Angleterre et aux États Unis.* Paris: Librairie Guillaumin and Cie.
Schumpeter, Joseph A. [1934] 1980. *Theory of Economic Development.* New York: Oxford University Press.
Somary, Felix. 1955. *Erinnerungen aus meinem Leben.* Zurich: Manesse.
Sombart, Werner. 1904. "Versuch einer Systematik der Wirtschaftskrise." *Archiv für Sozialwissenschaft und Sozialpolitik* 19:1–21.
Streissler, Erich. 1981. "Schumpeter's Vienna and the Role of Credit in Innovation." In *Schumpeterian Economics,* ed. Helmut Frisch. Eastbourne, East Sussex: Praeger.

Joseph Schumpeter: Radical Economist

Nathan Rosenberg

1

This paper will deal with the book, *Capitalism, Socialism and Democracy,* as the mature statement of the most radical scholar in the discipline of economics in the twentieth century.

Of course, I do not mean to suggest that Joseph Schumpeter held views on the organization of the economy, or society generally, that make it appropriate to label him as a radical in the political sense. In his social and political views, Schumpeter was anything but radical. In fact, one could make a case—although I do not propose to make it—that Schumpeter was not merely conservative in his social views, but reactionary. In his most private thoughts, as suggested by a recent biography, he seemed to possess an insatiable longing for the glorious later days of the Hapsburg monarchy. Moreover, the most charitable characterization of his attitude towards Nazi Germany in the darkest days of the 1930s and the Second World War is that he was ambivalent.

The reason I propose to call Schumpeter a radical is that he urged the rejection of the most central and precious tenets of neoclassical theory. Indeed, I want to insist that very little of the complex edifice of neoclassical economics, as it existed in the late 1930s and 1940s, survived the sweep of Schumpeter's devastating assaults. But in examining Schumpeter's criticism, it is not my primary intention to enlist his authority in an attack upon neoclassical economics. Rather, it is my intention to show that the quintessential later Schumpeter, the author of *Capitalism, Socialism and Democracy,* held views that were not only genuinely radical, but that are deserving of far more serious attention than they receive today, even, or perhaps especially, from scholars who think of themselves as working within the Schumpeterian tradition.

The main focus of this paper, as expected, will be on *Capitalism, Socialism and Democracy,* a great book whose publication, fifty years ago, we properly celebrate. Inevitably, however, it will also be necessary to draw upon some of Schumpeter's other writings in order to round out the interpretation of the book that I propose to place before you.

2

I can think of no more appropriate way to begin my presentation, here in Kyoto, than by quoting from Schumpeter's preface to the Japanese edition of his earlier book, *The Theory of Economic Development.* For in that preface, Schumpeter sketches out what is probably the most precise and succinct statement of his own intellectual agenda that he ever committed to print. That agenda focuses not only upon the understanding of how the economic system generates economic change, but on how that change occurs *as a result of the working out of purely endogenous forces.*

> If my Japanese readers asked me before opening the book what it is that I was aiming at when I wrote it, more than a quarter of a century ago, I would answer that I was trying to construct a theoretic model of the process of economic change in time, or perhaps more clearly, to answer the question how the economic system generates the force which incessantly transforms it. . . . I felt very strongly that . . . there was a source of energy within the economic system which would of itself disrupt any equilibrium that might be attained. If this is so, then there must be a purely economic theory of economic change which does not merely rely on external factors propelling the economic system from one equilibrium to another. It is such a theory that I have tried to build . . .[1]

It should be noted that these words were published in 1937, when Schumpeter was, as we know, already at work on *Capitalism, Socialism and Democracy.* In fact, I regard *Capitalism, Socialism and Democracy* as the fulfillment of precisely the intellectual agenda that Schumpeter articulated in the passage to his Japanese readers that I have just quoted.

Of course, an account of how and why economic change took place was precisely something that could not be provided within the "rigorously static" framework of neoclassical equilibrium analysis, as Schumpeter referred to it. Schumpeter also observed that it was Walras's view that economic theory was only capable of examining a "stationary process," that is, "a process which *actually* does not change of its own

---

1. Joseph A. Schumpeter, Preface to *Keigaihatten no riron* (translation of *Theorie Der Wirtschaftlichen Entwicklung* , Tokyo: Iwanami-Shoten, 1937), 1–3.

initiative, but merely produces constant rates of real income as it flows along in time." As Schumpeter interprets Walras:

> He would have said, (and, as a matter of fact, he did say it to me the only time that I had the opportunity to converse with him) that of course economic life is essentially passive and merely adapts itself to the natural and social influences which may be acting on it, so that the theory of a stationary process constitutes really the whole of theoretical economics and that as economic theorists we cannot say much about the factors that account for historical change, but must simply register them.[2]

The critical point here is that Schumpeter directly rejects the view of Walras that economic theory must be confined to the study of the stationary process, and that it cannot go farther than demonstrating how departures from equilibrium, such as might be generated by a growth in population or in savings, merely set into motion forces that restore the system to an equilibrium path. In proposing to develop a theory showing how a stationary process can be disturbed by internal, as well as external, forces, Schumpeter is suggesting that the essence of capitalism lies, not in equilibrating forces, but in the inevitable tendency of that system to *depart* from equilibrium—in a word, to disequilibrate. Equilibrium analysis fails to capture the essence of capitalist reality. Lest there should be any doubt about Schumpeter's position on this critical matter, we cite his own forceful formulation: "Whereas a stationary feudal economy would still be a feudal economy, and a stationary socialist economy would still be a socialist economy, stationary capitalism is a contradiction in terms."[3]

Although Schumpeter did, in fact, make important use of Walrasian general equilibrium in his analysis of the circular flow in a stationary state, he used the concept precisely as a means of demonstrating how capitalist economies would behave *if they were deprived of their essential feature:* that is, innovative activities that are the primary generator of economic change.

It is important to understand the methodological use that Schumpeter makes of the neoclassical analysis of a stationary economic process. As Schumpeter stated: "In appraising the performance of competitive enterprise, the question whether it would or would not tend to

---

2. Schumpeter, *Theorie*, 2–3.
3. Joseph A. Schumpeter, "Capitalism in the Postwar World," in *Essays of J. A. Schumpeter*, ed. R. Clemence, Cambridge, Mass.: Addison-Wesley, 1951, 174.

maximize production in a perfectly equilibrated stationary condition of the economic process is . . . almost, though not quite, irrelevant."[4]

The reason that it is not completely irrelevant is that the model of a stationary competitive process helps to understand the behavior of an economy that possesses no internal forces generating economic change. Thus, the model of a Walrasian circular flow constitutes Schumpeter's starting point in understanding the essential elements of capitalist reality, because it shows how the system would behave in the absence of its most distinctive feature—innovation. It is an invaluable abstraction precisely because it makes it possible to trace out with greater precision the impact of innovative activity. This is the role served by the Walrasian conception of the circular flow in Schumpeter's analysis of business cycles, as well as growth.

Of course, one can always adopt the position that Schumpeter and neoclassical economics address very different questions, and that the theoretical analysis of each is valid in its particular intellectual context. Newton's law of gravity, after all, was not invalidated by Mendeleev's periodic table of the elements. Each theory was devised to account for different classes of phenomena. They do not contradict each other and they may, therefore, be simultaneously valid—or invalid.

I believe that there is something to be said in support of such a position. But I am not at all confident that the Schumpeter of Part 2 of *Capitalism, Socialism and Democracy* would have been satisfied with it. Schumpeter's position seems to be that, if you want to understand what capitalism is all about as an economic system, the fundamental question is how it generates economic change, rather than how it restores stability. Not all theoretical frameworks are equally useful in analyzing the essential feature of modern capitalism. And again, the essential feature, in Schumpeter's view, is economic change. This is because the capitalist form of economic organization has a built-in logic that dominates the behavior of that economic system. Thus, economists who purport to have something to say that is pertinent to the contemporary operation of capitalism have the obligation to deal with certain distinctive patterns of capitalist behavior and to explain their consequences. The behavior of capitalism is totally dominated by the continual working out of its inner logic, the essence of which is economic change resulting from the impact of the innovation process.

Equilibrium analysis, on the other hand, focuses upon adjustment mechanisms that are only peripheral, and not central, to the logic of capitalist organization and incentives. Therefore, a theoretical approach

---

4. Schumpeter, *Capitalism,* 77.

that neglects persistent disequilibrium, instability, and growth is an approach that deals with processes that are, at best, phenomena of secondary importance, or only mere epiphenomena.[5]

3

I do not propose to examine in any detail Schumpeter's views on innovation, or the breadth of his definition of innovation, since these are familiar to all readers of his major works. I do, however, propose to underline the rather radical implications that Schumpeter himself drew from the primacy that he attached to innovation—implications that have received little attention.

The dynamic forces that are inherent in the capitalist structure lead Schumpeter to treat capitalism as a system whose essential feature is an evolutionary process and not the mechanisms that force the system to revert to an equilibrium after some external force has produced a small departure from that equilibrium. For those who find the term "disequilibrium analysis" too paradoxical to be useful as a description of Schumpeter's mode of economic analysis, I suggest the propriety of the term "evolutionary." My justification is a simple one: It is Schumpeter's own frequently used term in *Capitalism, Socialism and Democracy.*

> The essential point to grasp is that in dealing with capitalism we are dealing with an evolutionary process. . . . Capitalism . . . is by nature a form or method of economic change and not only never is but never can be stationary. And this evolutionary character of the capitalist process is not merely due to the fact that economic life goes on in a social and natural environment which changes and by its changes alters the data of economic action; this fact is important and these changes (wars, revolutions and so on) often condition industrial change, but they are not its prime movers. Nor is this evolutionary character due to a quasi-automatic increase in population and capital or to the vagaries of monetary systems of which exactly the same thing holds true.[6]

I ask readers of *Capitalism, Socialism and Democracy* to ponder the far-reaching implications of this statement. For it involves not only

---

5. For a perceptive examination of the limits of equilibrium analysis in the context of innovation studies, see Richard R. Nelson, "Schumpeter and Contemporary Research on the Economics of Innovation," Columbia University, February 1992.

6. Schumpeter, *Capitalism,* 82. See also ibid., 58.

the recognition of the inherently dynamic nature of capitalism. It also involves nothing less than the rejection of the competitive ideal itself, as that ideal is enshrined not only in economist's models, but also in decades of government regulation and, in the United States, in a full century of antitrust legislation. In this view, textbook competition is not an ideal state to be pursued. The welfare implications of the competitive ideal reflect a mistaken preoccupation with the distinctly secondary issue of how the economy allocates an existing stock of resources; whereas the far more significant concern for Schumpeter is how successful an economic system is at generating growth—growth in a qualitative as well as a quantitative sense. In my own reading, this deserves to be regarded as the central message of *Capitalism, Socialism and Democracy*. Capitalists survive, if they survive at all, by learning to live in, and to participate in, a "perennial gale of creative destruction. . . . The problem that is usually being visualized is how capitalism administers existing structures, whereas the relevant problem is how it creates and destroys them" (84). I call attention to the significant fact that Schumpeter attached so much importance to this last observation that he repeated it, almost verbatim, in the preface to the second edition of *Capitalism, Socialism and Democracy*.

In my view, if one is looking for a distinctively "Schumpeterian hypothesis," it lies in this definition of the essential nature of the competitive process. Perhaps this should not be regarded as a hypothesis, since it is difficult to reduce it to a testable, potentially refutable form. It is more in the nature of a conception or, better, to use a favorite Schumpeterian term, a "vision" of the essential nature of capitalism. It is a vision in which it is a mistake to reduce monopoly to the purely restrictive and antisocial consequences that are normally ascribed to it, since monopoly power is often a temporary adjunct of the process of creative destruction. The Schumpeter of *Capitalism, Socialism and Democracy* does indeed attach considerable significance to the growth in the absolute size of the firm in the course of the twentieth century. At the same time, I would like to insist that a "Schumpeterian hypothesis," which postulates a strong association between market power and innovation, is an extreme oversimplification of a much more sophisticated—and much more radical—view of the meaning of competition.[7]

Thus, Schumpeter is involved in an explicit rejection of the central neoclassical notion that atomistic competition offers unique welfare advantages. In *Capitalism, Socialism and Democracy*, he posits a novel

---

7. See Nelson, "Schumpeter and Contemporary Research," for an illuminating discussion of this issue.

conception of competition based upon innovation as a central element in a disequilibrium process that leads the economy to higher levels of income, output, and, presumably, well-being. In the course of the twentieth century, the large-scale firm, with its internal research capabilities, has become the dominant engine of technical progress. This is a main theme of *Capitalism, Socialism and Democracy,* as opposed to his earlier book, *The Theory of Economic Development.* Schumpeter's argument is certainly closely tied to bigness and to the dismissal of the virtues of perfect competition. It recognizes some degree of monopoly power as a passing phase of the innovation process. But rejecting the virtues of perfect competition is not the same thing as saying that monopoly power is inherently favorable to innovation.

> Thus it is not sufficient to argue that because perfect competition is impossible under modern industrial conditions—or because it always has been impossible—the large-scale establishment or unit of control must be accepted as a necessary evil inseparable from the economic progress which it is prevented from sabotaging by the forces inherent in its productive apparatus. What we have got to accept is that it has come to be the most powerful engine of that progress and in particular of the long-run expansion of total output not only in spite of, but to a considerable extent through, this strategy which looks so restrictive when viewed in the individual case and from the individual point of time. In this respect, perfect competition is not only impossible but inferior, and has no title to being set up as a model of ideal efficiency.[8]

Indeed, the perennial gale of creative destruction is continually sweeping away the entrenched monopoly power that appeared so secure until a new innovation consigned it to the scrapheap of history. That is precisely why the perennial gale is such a critically important economic force.

4

But there is much more to Schumpeter the radical antineoclassicist than has been suggested so far. This becomes apparent as soon as it is recognized that innovation, the central feature of capitalist reality, is not a product of a decisionmaking process that can be described or analyzed as "rational."

---

8. Schumpeter, *Capitalism,* 106.

The assumption that business behavior is ideally rational and prompt, and also that in principle it is the same with all firms, works tolerably well only within the precincts of tried experience and familiar motive. It breaks down as soon as we leave those precincts and allow the business community under study to be faced by—not simply new situations, which also occur as soon as external factors unexpectedly intrude but by—new possibilities of business action which are as yet untried and about which the most complete command of routine teaches nothing. Those differences in the behaviour of different people which within those precincts account for secondary phenomena only, become essential in the sense that they now account for the outstanding features of reality and that a picture drawn on the Walras-Marshallian lines ceases to be true—even in the qualified sense in which it is true of stationary and growing processes: it misses those features, and becomes wrong in the endeavor to account by means of its own analysis for phenomena which the assumptions of that analysis exclude.[9]

It is, of course, difficult to imagine a more profound rejection of neoclassical economics than is embodied in Schumpeter's forceful assertion that the most important feature of capitalist reality—innovation—is one to which rational decision making has no direct application. The nature of the innovation process, the drastic departure from existing routines, is inherently one that cannot be reduced to mere calculation, although subsequent imitation of the innovation, once accomplished, can be so reduced. Innovation is the creation of knowledge that cannot, and therefore should not, be "anticipated" by the theorist in a purely formal manner, as is done in the theory of decision making under uncertainty. In Schumpeter's view, it would be entirely meaningless to speak of "the future state of the world," as that state is not merely unknown, but also indefinable in empirical and historical terms. Serious doubt is thus cast on what meaning, if any, can be possessed by intertemporal models of equilibrium under uncertainty, in which the essential nature of innovation is systematically neglected.

Thus, if rationality is reduced in the neoclassical world more and more to the tautology that people do the best they can, given the whole gamut of constraints they face (among the most important of which is the informational constraint), then accepting Schumpeter's concept of innovation means that human actions are always second best, in a way that ultimately

---

9. Joseph A. Schumpeter, *Business Cycles*, Vol. 1 (New York: McGraw-Hill Book Company, 1939), 98–99.

cannot be subjected to further analysis. For rational behavior, in Schumpeter's view, is most significant in a world of routine and repetition of similar events. (Needless to say, the modern literature on rational expectations does not overcome Schumpeter's strictures here. The "rationality" of rational expectations is limited by currently available information, and, thus, the inherent uncertainty concerning the future is not eliminated.)

But this is not the end of Schumpeter's rather complex treatment of the role of rationality. If one considers rationality in the long historical context, Schumpeter mounts an argument in *Capitalism, Socialism and Democracy,* the essential element of which is that capitalism, considered as a civilization, has continuously enlarged the social space within which rationalistic attitudes and habits of thought come to prevail. In chapter 11, "The Civilization of Capitalism," Schumpeter argues that capitalism has expanded the sphere within which "rational cost-profit calculations" could be carried out. Moreover,

primarily a product of the evolution of economic rationality, the cost-profit calculus in turn reacts upon that rationality; by crystallizing and defining numerically, it powerfully propels the logic of enterprise. And thus defined and quantified for the economic sector, this type of logic or attitude or method then starts upon its conqueror's career, subjugating—rationalizing—man's tools and philosophies, his medical practice, his picture of the cosmos, his outlook on life, everything in fact including his concepts of beauty and justice and his spiritual ambitions. . . . (123–24)

This aspect of Schumpeter's argument—what he himself might have described as his own "economic sociology"—is, in my opinion, analytically brilliant, breathtaking in its sweep, and, historically, substantially correct. I regret that it is impossible here to examine his argument in detail. I remind you of it now because it is the linchpin to Schumpeter's argument that capitalism will eventually "self-destruct." The self-destruction is inevitable because, in his view, the historical expansion of rationality brings in its wake two crucial consequences.

The first is that rationality challenges and unfrocks beliefs and institutions that cannot survive the searching and corrosive glare of a (presumably narrow) rationality: "When the habit of rational analysis of, and rational behavior in, the daily tasks of life has gone far enough, it turns back upon the mass of collective ideas and criticizes and to some extent 'rationalizes' them by way of such questions as why there should be kings and popes or subordination or tithes or property" (122).

The second consequence is that, as capitalism expands the sphere to which rationality applies, it eventually learns how to supplant the entrepreneur, the human "carrier" of innovation, with institutions that do away with the social leadership of the entrepreneur himself. The entrepreneurial function itself becomes rationalized—or bureaucratized—with the growth of the large firm. "For . . . it is now much easier than it has been in the past to do things that lie outside familiar routine—innovation itself has been reduced to routine. Technological progress is increasingly becoming the business of teams of trained specialists who turn out what is required and make it work in predictable ways" (132).

Of course, the growth of large-scale enterprise and the "obsolescence of the entrepreneurial function" led Schumpeter, through the rich argument of his economic and political sociology, to his conclusion that capitalism could not survive. The ideology and social myths that once sustained it could not survive its tendency to "automatize progress" (134) and, thus, to reveal its new-found ability to do without the leadership and vitality once provided by the entrepreneur and the bourgeoisie.

My own view—with the easy wisdom of fifty years of retrospection—is that Schumpeter much overstated the extent to which technological progress would become automatized. I believe that this, in turn, is partly due to his intensive focus upon the earliest stages in the innovation process, and to his failure to consider the degree to which commercial success is dependent upon subsequent stages in the carrying out of an innovation. But, regrettably, these issues cannot be explored here. What is essential to my examination of Schumpeter the radical is the observation that both in the past and in the future, it is Schumpeter's view that a rational approach to the innovation process is incompatible with capitalist institutions. So long as the function is carried out by the individual entrepreneur, it is an act based upon intuition and charismatic leadership; when capitalist institutions eventually, at some future date, succeed in subjecting innovation to a rationalized routine, those institutions will, ipso facto, lose their luster and social justification, and be replaced by a socialized state.

Thus, in a world where capitalist institutions continue to prevail, innovation calls upon a decision-making process that goes beyond rational calculation. When capitalist development eventually leads to the institutionalization of innovation, the organizational basis of the economy will, Schumpeter believes, be transformed into some form of socialism. In neither case, ironically, does Schumpeter concede a significant role for the neoclassical analysis of rational behavior.

5

Schumpeter's radical antineoclassical stance extends even to the issue of what it is that constitutes the explicanda of economic analysis. It is normal practice for neoclassical economists to take tastes and technology as exogenously given, and to seek to examine issues of resource allocation by explicit reference to changes in incomes and relative prices.[10]

Thus, Schumpeter's assault on neoclassical economics includes even his deliberate violation of the sanctum sanctorum of the neoclassical citadel: the commitments to the exogeneity of consumer preferences and the associated virtues of consumer sovereignty. His belief that the central problem of the economist is to account for economic change over time undoubtedly played an important role in sharpening his perception of the forces influencing consumer preferences.

> Innovations in the economic system do not as a rule take place in such a way that first new wants arise spontaneously in consumers and then the productive apparatus swings round through their pressure. We do not deny the presence of this nexus. It is, however, the producer who as a rule initiates economic change, and consumers are educated by him if necessary; they are, as it were, taught to want new things, or things which differ in some respect or other from those which they have been in the habit of using. Therefore, while it is permissible and even necessary to consider consumers' wants as an independent and indeed the fundamental force in a theory of the circular flow, we must take a different attitude as soon as we analyze *change*.[11]

Schumpeter made the same essential point later on in *Business Cycles:*

> We will, throughout, act on the assumption that consumers' initiative in changing their tastes—i.e., in changing that set of our data which general theory comprises in the concepts of "utility functions" or "indifference varieties"—is negligible and that all change in consumers' tastes is incident to, and brought about by, producers' actions. This requires both justification and qualification. The fact on which we stand is, of course, common knowledge. Railroads have not emerged because any consumers took the initiative in displaying an effective demand for their service in preference to

---

10. See George Stigler and Gary Becker, "De Gustibus non est Disputandum," *American Economic Review* 67 (1977): 76–90.

11. Joseph A. Schumpeter, *The Theory of Economic Development* (Cambridge, Mass.: Harvard University Press, 1949), 65. Emphasis Schumpeter's. [First published in German in 1911].

the services of mail coaches. Nor did the consumers display any such initiative and wish to have electric lamps or rayon stockings, or to travel by motorcar or airplane, or to listen to radios, or to chew gum. There is obviously no lack of realism in the proposition that the great majority of changes in commodities consumed has been forced by producers on consumers who, more often than not, have resisted the change and have had to be educated up by elaborate psychotechnics of advertising. (73)

Although modern economists have, of course, investigated the consequences of endogenous preferences for welfare judgments, most have considered it better, for reasons of division of labor with other disciplines, in particular psychology, to neglect the investigation of why and how tastes change.[12] But Schumpeter asserted that innovation, the fundamental driving force of the historical evolution of capitalism, would mold tastes, as well as technology, in unexpected ways. The implications, for the development of the economic and social systems, as well as for microeconomic welfare judgments, were, as Schumpeter recognized, potentially radical. Just before his death in 1950, he severely criticized economists for "the uncritical belief that so many seem to harbour in the virtues of consumer's choice":

First of all, whether we like it or not, we are witnessing a momentous experiment in malleability of tastes—is not this worth analyzing? Second, ever since the physiocrats (and before), economists have professed unbounded respect for the consumers' choice—is it not time to investigate what the bases for this respect are and how far the traditional and, in part, advertisement-shaped tastes of people are subject to the qualification that they might prefer other things than those which they want at present as soon as they have acquired familiarity with these other things? In matters of education, health, and housing there is already practical unanimity about this—but might the principle not be carried much further? Third, economic theory accepts existing tastes as data, no matter whether it postulates utility functions or indifference varieties or simply preference directions, and these data are made the starting point of price theory. Hence, they must be considered as independent of prices. But considerable and persistent changes in prices obviously do react upon tastes. *What, then, is to become of our theory and the*

---

12. See, for example, Milton Friedman, *Price Theory* (New York: Aldine Publishing Company, 1976), 13.

whole of micro-economics? It is investigations of this kind, that might break new ground, which I miss.[13]

The earlier discussion of Schumpeter's analysis of innovation has already anticipated his unwillingness to treat technological change, as well as consumers' tastes, as an exogenous phenomenon. But it is necessary to distinguish between the earlier Schumpeter of the *Theory of Economic Development* (1911) and the later Schumpeter of *Capitalism, Socialism and Democracy* (1942). In his earlier book, Schumpeter looked upon invention as an exogenous activity and upon innovation as endogenous. Whereas inventors conducted their activities off the economic stage and contributed their artifacts to a pool of invention, the timing of the entrepreneurial decision to draw from this pool was decisively shaped by economic forces. But the later Schumpeter saw both invention and innovation as generated by economic forces inside the large firm with its own internal research capabilities. The reason for the change in Schumpeter's views during this period is not far to seek: the economic world, the object of Schumpeter's studies, had changed substantially during the period between the publication of the two books. Schumpeter's altered views were an acknowledgment of the empirical changes that had occurred during his own professional lifetime.

Schumpeter's insistence upon the role of endogenous forces applies, not only to technology, but also to science itself. The rationalizing influence of the capitalistic mentality and institutions created "the growth of rational science," as well as its "long list of applications" (125). Significantly, Schumpeter cites as examples not only "Airplanes, refrigerators, television and that sort of thing . . ." but also the "modern hospital." Although one might be surprised at the appearance here of an institution that is not commonly operated on a profitmaking basis, Schumpeter's explanation is illuminating. It is

fundamentally because capitalist rationality supplied the habits of mind that evolved the methods used in these hospitals. And the victories, not yet completely won but in the offing, over cancer, syphilis and tuberculosis will be as much capitalist achievements as motorcars or pipe lines or Bessemer steel have been. In the case of medicine, there is a capitalist profession behind the methods, capitalist both because to a large extent it works in a business spirit and because it is an emulsion of the industrial and commercial bourgeoi-

---

13. Joseph A. Schumpeter, "English Economists and the State-Managed Economy," *Journal of Political Economy* 57, no. 5 (1949): 380–81; emphasis Schumpeter's.

sie. But even if that were not so, modern medicine and hygiene would still be by-products of the capitalist process just as is modern education. (125–26)

Thus, Schumpeter insists that both science and technology, normally so far from the world of phenomena examined by neoclassical economics, are, in reality, highly endogenous to the economic world, subject to the gravitational pull of economic forces. In one of the last articles published during his own lifetime, Schumpeter identified his own views with those of Marx on the role played by Western capitalism in accounting for progress in both science and technology. Schumpeter observed that Marx had, in the *Communist Manifesto,* "launched out on a panegyric upon bourgeois achievement that has no equal in economic literature." After quoting a relevant portion of the text, he says:

> No reputable "bourgeois" economist of that or any other time— certainly not A. Smith or J. S. Mill—ever said as much as this. Observe, in particular, the emphasis upon the creative role of the business class that the majority of the most "bourgeois" economists so persistently overlooked and of the business class as such, whereas most of us would, on the one hand, also insert into the picture non-bourgeois contributions to the bourgeois success—the contributions of non-bourgeois bureaucracies, for instance—and, on the other hand, commit the mistake (for such I believe it is) to list as independent factors science and technology, whereas Marx's sociology enabled him to see that these as well as "progress" in such fields as education and hygiene were just as much the products of the bourgeois culture—hence, ultimately, of the business class—as was the business performance itself.[14]

Did Schumpeter, then, believe, along with Marx, in the economic interpretation of history? I suggest that he did, with certain qualifications. However, the qualifications that Schumpeter imposed upon the economic interpretation of history were of a sort that, if anything, actually strengthened its usefulness as a device for explaining economic change. It is important here to recall that the first four chapters of *Capitalism, Socialism and Democracy* are devoted entirely to an examination of Marx's views on a range of subjects. Schumpeter offered a

---

14. Joseph A. Schumpeter, "The Communist Manifesto in Sociology and Economics," *Journal of Political Economy* 57, no. 3 (1949): 293. See also Schumpeter, *Capitalism,* chap. 1.

sympathetic and approving treatment of the economic interpretation of history; moreover, almost all of his own writing fits conveniently into that interpretation. But Schumpeter also compresses the economic interpretation into just two propositions:

1. The forms or conditions of production are the fundamental determinants of social structures, which, in turn, breed attitudes, actions, and civilizations.
2. The forms of production themselves have a logic of their own; that is to say, they change according to necessities inherent in them so as to produce their successors merely by their own working. (11–12)

Schumpeter asserts that "Both propositions undoubtedly contain a large amount of truth and are, as we shall find at several turns of our way, invaluable working hypotheses" (12). His main qualification, if that is what it really is, is his insistence upon the importance of lags—that is, social forms that persist after they have lost their economic rationale. It is far from clear that Marx would have disagreed with such a qualification, since Marx was much too sophisticated a historian to believe that economic changes generated the "appropriate" social changes instantaneously. Schumpeter, in making the qualification about lags, adds that Marx, although perhaps not fully appreciating their implications, would not have taken the simplistic position involved in denying them a role.

> Social structures, types and attitudes are coins that do not readily melt. Once they are formed they persist, possibly for centuries, and since different structures and types display different degrees of this ability to survive, we almost always find that actual group and national behaviour more or less departs from what we should expect it to be if we tried to infer it from the dominant forms of the productive process. Though this applies quite generally, it is most clearly seen when a highly durable structure transfers itself bodily from one country to another. The social situation created in Sicily by the Norman conquest will illustrate my meaning. Such facts Marx did not overlook but he hardly realized all their implications. (12–13)

6

Whether or not one concludes, as I do, that Schumpeter believed in a form of the economic interpretation of history, he clearly was strongly committed to the view that economic phenomena, in order to be meaningfully examined, must be studied in a historical context. Since I have spent a significant portion of my own professional life studying economic behavior in historical contexts, I am naturally pleased to be able to invoke the authority of Schumpeter in support of such an approach. At the same time, I believe that this interpretation of Schumpeter is more than merely a self-serving exercise on my part.

The fact is that most of what Schumpeter wrote qualifies as history, both economic and intellectual. Not only *Capitalism, Socialism and Democracy,* but, in addition, *Business Cycles* and his posthumous *History of Economic Analysis* are historical works. His commitment to the historical approach was deeply rooted in his thought. Schumpeter had a profound appreciation for the path-dependent nature of economic phenomena and, therefore, of economic analysis itself. More than this, the very subject matter of economics, in Schumpeter's view, is history. Economics is about economic change as it has occurred over historical time. That is why he insisted upon the importance of studying capitalism as an evolutionary process. It is also why he assigned such a limited importance to the study of stationary economic processes. And these things have a great deal to do with Schumpeter's highest regard for some of Marx's contributions to economic analysis.

> There is . . . one thing of fundamental importance for the methodology of economics which he actually achieved. Economists always have either themselves done work in economic history or else used the historical work of others. But the facts of economic history were assigned to a separate compartment. They entered theory, if at all, merely in the role of illustrations, or possibly of verifications of results. They mixed with it only mechanically. Now Marx's mixture is a chemical one; that is to say, he introduced them into the very argument that produces the results. He was the first economist of top rank to see and to teach systematically how economic theory may be turned into historical analysis and how the historical narrative may be turned into *histoire raisonnee.*[15]

This passage, it seems to me, is also the best explanation for Schumpeter's frequent expression of admiration for, and intellectual indebtedness to, Marx.

I can think of no better way of closing than by reminding you of certain views that Schumpeter expressed in chapter 2 of his *History of Economic Analysis.* After stating that a "scientific" economist is to be

---

15. Schumpeter, *Capitalism,* 44.

identified by the demonstrated command over three techniques—history, statistics, and theory—he goes on to say:

> Of these fundamental fields, economic history—which issues into and includes present-day facts—is by far the most important. I wish to state right now that if, starting my work in economics afresh, I were told that I could study only one of the three but could have my choice, it would be economic history that I should choose. And this on three grounds. First, the subject matter of economics is essentially a unique process in historic time. Nobody can hope to understand the economic phenomena of any, including the present, epoch who has not an adequate command of historical *facts* and an adequate amount of historical *sense* or of what may be described as *historical experience*. Second, the historical report cannot be purely economic but must inevitably reflect also "institutional" facts that are not purely economic; therefore it affords the best method for understanding how economic and non-economic facts are related to one another and how the various social sciences *should* be related to one another. Third, it is, I believe, the fact that most of the fundamental errors currently committed in economic analysis are due to a lack of historical experience more often than to any other shortcoming of the economist's equipment. . . . (12–13; emphasis Schumpeter's)

It is sad to have to conclude with the observation that some knowledge of history is still not regarded as essential to competent economic analysis. Indeed, judging by the curricula of the graduate programs in U.S. universities today, the very idea would appear to be distinctly perverse and alien. In this, as in so many other respects, Schumpeter the radical economist still has a great deal to teach us.

Commentary

Laurence S. Moss

I have three criticisms to make of Professor Rosenberg's stimulating paper:

First Criticism

On page 1, Professor Rosenberg promises to focus on *Capitalism, Socialism and Democracy* (CSD). He explains that other sources will be used, but only to "round out" the interpretation of that book. In this first criticism, I hold him to that promise.

In section 4, Rosenberg takes up Schumpeter's interesting claim that, in addition to innovating, the entrepreneur is often a "teacher" and "educator" of consumers. The claim appears in his 1912 *Theory of Economic Development* and is repeated again in the first volume of *Business Cycles* (1939). Schumpeter argues that the entrepreneur not only pioneers new combinations of resources, but, in order to be successful, must communicate his or her findings to consumers. Schumpeter considers this an educational process. Unlike the Austrian treatment of the coordinating entrepreneur who (mostly) anticipates future market conditions and prepares for those conditions by speculating about how resources can be used more profitably, Schumpeter's entrepreneur is out there actually changing the shape of business history by molding, shaping, and perhaps creating consumer demand.

This raises at least two questions. The first is whether what Schumpeter said in 1912, and again in 1939, is compatible with traditional or orthodox price theory. As K. Lancaster (1971) has shown, it is perfectly possible to interpret the behavior of entrepreneurs as simply pioneering new combinations of known product characteristics. The entrepreneur merely educates consumers about the new possibilities for consumption, and they decide, on the basis of income and relative prices, whether they are worthwhile for purchase. Thus, a new automobile may contain safety brakes, a telephone, a fax machine, and a CD player, and this new combination must be marketed and promoted. My concern here is with who is educating whom about what and whether the phenomenon of entrepreneur-as-educator really represents a radical departure from orthodox price theory, as Rosenberg maintains.

This brings me to my second question: What new material did Schumpeter provide in CSD to clarify the problem of entrepreneur-as-educator? It is totally fair that I present Rosenberg with this challenge. Indeed, he stated that his purpose in this paper was to "focus" on CSD and only bring in material from Schumpeter's other major writings if it helped illuminate CSD. It would be interesting to know how, and to what extent, Schumpeter extended the 1912 and 1939, respective, discussions of entrepreneur-as-educator in the 1942 book. Is the problem discussed at all in CSD? If the phenomenon is not discussed at all in CSD, then what does this suggest to us about the significance of the phenomenon to Schumpeter himself? Would CSD be a better book had it contained some discussion of the entrepreneur-as-educator?

Second Criticism

Rosenberg's principal thesis is that Schumpeter was a "radical," because he rejected orthodox price theory and, instead, championed a more dynamic price theory. By "dynamic," Rosenberg means a theory that focuses on the information prices provide about changing market conditions. In defense of his thesis, Rosenberg is required to offer some discussion of two related issues.

First, it would be useful and important in assessing Schumpeter's originality to have a more complete description of the "state of the arts" in the economic literature circa 1930 and 1940. How novel and unusual was Schumpeter's position, for its time?

Apparently, the attack on competition as a "state of affairs" already had a distinguished history that must have been familiar to Schumpeter when he wrote CSD. There was, of course, J. M. Clark's "Toward a Concept of Workable Competition," which appeared in the *American Economic Review* in 1940 and, along with Schumpeter, exerted an enormous influence on postwar German competition policy, as Wolfgang Kerber has recently argued. Leopold von Wiese's *"Die Konkurrenz, vorwiegent in soziologisch-systematischer Betrachtung"* called attention to the experimental nature of competition in 1929—more than a year before Schumpeter started writing CSD. Other pioneering dissenters whose attacks on using the idea of perfect competition as a blueprint for reforming the economy include E. Chamberlin, L. von Mises, and F. A.

Hayek. Additional sources for Schumpeter's ideas about competition are also provided by Professor Streissler, in his conference paper (in this volume).

My point is not to belittle Schumpeter's contribution or suggest that Rosenberg overstated Schumpeter's originality. Rather, Rosenberg should provide a more complete treatment of the intellectual backdrop against which Schumpeter first presented his ideas about competition and competition policy in 1942.

The second matter that I think deserves more attention is a technical question about theory. When Schumpeter discarded the model of perfect competition, what was it that he intended to put into its place? After all, when Schumpeter announced, in the third part of CSD, that socialism could work, he cast his vote in favor of O. Lange, F. Taylor, and Dickinson, and against Mises and Hayek. Perhaps Schumpeter was persuaded by Barone's mathematical reasoning about this scientific question. But the proof that relative market prices communicate important information about relative resource scarcity requires the equality between price and marginal cost, or at least some special assumptions about how much they differ throughout the economy.

In orthodox analysis, price theory is less a matter of competition as a process of discovery and utilization of information and more a highly technical device for establishing the claim that market prices balance supply and demand in all markets. In 1948, Hayek wrote what may also have been Schumpeter's considered opinion, that "competition is by its nature a dynamic process whose essential characteristics are assumed away by the assumptions underlying static analysis." This claim has produced one strong challenge.

In a recent paper, J. Eatwell and M. Milgate (E&M) specifically challenge those who would follow Hayek and Schumpeter and claim that competition is a dynamic discovery procedure to explain how markets can be shown to be "efficient" without the static results of the model of perfect competition. Citing Aumann's finding that "the notion of perfect competition is fundamental in the treatment of economic equilibrium" and noting that "dropping the assumption of perfect competition has very destructive consequences for neoclassical price theory," E&M ask what substitute concepts will be put in place. Surely this is especially a problem for Schumpeter, since he supported the liberal socialists in their claim that, by instructing managers to simulate the results of perfect competition, they would bring about an efficient economic result. Rosenberg might address himself to what appears to be something of an inconsistency in Schumpeter's CSD.

Third Criticism

Rosenberg makes much of Schumpeter's claims in CSD that innovation is not a product of rational decision making. In his early writings, Schumpeter treated innovation as something heroic, brought by eccentric men of vision who manage to stick to their resolve against all odds. To shake the masses from their coordinated routines requires bank credit, so that the resources can be wrested from their most "rational" applications to new applications that will, perhaps someday in the future, be seen as "rational," but only after time has passed and new routines established.

In CSD, innovation is described as every day becoming more "automatized" (Rosenberg's word) in the large corporation. If this were the case, then older capitalist institutions (such as bank credit creation) might lose their purpose and no longer be essential to capitalist development. Indeed, some form of socialism might be both possible and inevitable, now that innovation has itself become routinized. Rosenberg suggests that Schumpeter's appreciation of processes of technological change may have been less than satisfactory. According to Rosenberg:

> Schumpeter much overstated the extent to which technological progress would become automatized. I believe that this, in turn, is partly due to his intensive focus upon the earliest stages in the innovation process, and to his failure to consider the degree to which commercial success is dependent upon subsequent stages in the carrying out of an innovation. But, regrettably, these issues cannot be explored here.

I cannot let Professor Rosenberg off the hook so easily. Isn't the fiftieth anniversary of CSD the perfect occasion to explore the phenomenon of technological change?

More important, Professor Rosenberg is, himself, an expert about processes of technological change and how they contributed to the economic development of the West ahead of, say, Asia and Africa. In an important study published in 1985 under the title, *How the West Grew Rich: The Economic Transformation of the Industrial World,* Professor Rosenberg and Professor Birdzell (R&B) provided what I consider to be a stimulating answer to that difficult question.

According to R&B, the West grew rich first because its legal and cultural norms encouraged, rewarded, and protected "experimentation" in the arts, in the applied sciences, and, most importantly, in commerce.

In the nineteenth century, special forms of business organization that limited the personal liability of the investors also encouraged experimental risk taking or venturing. The design of property rights structures that permitted inventors and innovators to appropriate rents from their original business applications encouraged commercial experimentation and the development of industry. Even the law of liability for accidents in industry and on the roads and highways encouraged material progress in the West.

I am disappointed that Rosenberg has not taken this opportunity to reconcile his well-stated findings about those broad patterns of technological change to what Schumpeter said in CSD about the development of capitalism. Indeed, in the final sections of the paper, Rosenberg applauds Schumpeter's interest in economic history and the study of economic phenomena in a historical context. If, as Rosenberg argues, Schumpeter believed in an economic interpretation of history, is prodevelopmental institutional change endogenous or exogenous to the process of historical change? Perhaps the West grew rich ahead of other parts of the world because intellectual forces inspired and reconditioned men's minds to accept and construct the new legal structures. If ideas undergo evolutionary change first and only after that do institutions change, then what is left of Schumpeter's economic interpretation of history?

In short, I am optimistic that Rosenberg's "Schumpeter-Was-A-Radical" thesis can be developed more completely, especially if Rosenberg were to make more use of his own valuable findings about processes of technological change, and to relate them more closely to the argument of CSD. My disappointment is that Rosenberg has not taken this opportunity to at least reconcile his stimulating remarks here with his earlier, valuable work on technological change.

REFERENCES

Aumann, R. J. 1974. "Markets with a Continuum of Traders." *Econometrica* 32: 39–50.
Clark, J. M. 1940. "Toward a Concept of Workable Competition." *American Economic Review* 30, no. 2 (June): 241–56.
Eatwell, J., and M. Milgate. 1992. "The Problem of Price Determination and Hayek's Theory of Competition." Paper presented at Conference on the Economics of F. A. Hayek, July 1992, Forli, Italy.
Hayek, Friedrich A. 1949. "The Meaning of Competition." First presented as a lecture in 1946, in idem, *Individualism and Economic Order*. London: Routledge and Kegan.

Hayek, Friedrich A. 1976. "Competition as a Discovery Procedure." First presented as a lecture in 1968, in idem, *New Studies in Philosophy, Politics, Economics and the History of Ideas.* Chicago: University of Chicago.

Jessua, C. "CSD after 50 Years: Why Did Schumpeter's Predictions Fail?" Paper presented at the Kyoto Conference of the International Joseph A. Schumpeter Society.

Kerber, Wolfgang. 1992. "German Market Process Theory." (March 1992).

Lancaster, K. 1971. *Consumer Demand: A New Approach.* New York: Columbia University Press.

Rosenberg, N., and L. E. Birdzell, Jr. 1986. *How the West Grew Rich: The Economic Transformation of the Industrial World.* New York: Basic Books.

Streissler, Erich W. "The Influence of German and Austrian Economics on Joseph A. Schumpeter." Paper presented at the Kyoto Conference of the International Joseph A. Schumpeter Society. In this volume.

Wiese, L. von. 1929. "Die Konkurrenz, vorswiegend in soziologisch-systematischer Bertrachtung." *Verhandlungen des 6. Deutschen Soziologentages.* Cited in Hayek 1976, 179, n. 1.

The Concept of the Tax State in Modern Public Finance Analysis

Jürgen G. Backhaus

Introduction

Schumpeter's student, Paul A. Samuelson, shortly after Schumpeter's death, gave public finance theory a direction and purpose that it has still kept, and that can help us explain why the concept of the tax state must appear elusive to the modern public finance expert. In his renowned article "The Pure Theory of Public Expenditure," Samuelson (1954, 387) matter-of-factly asserts:

> Except for Sax, Wicksell, Lindahl, Musgrave, and Bowen, econo-mists have rather neglected the theory of optimal public expendi-ture, spending most of their energy on the theory of taxation. There-fore, I explicitly assume two categories of goods: ordinary *private consumption goods* . . . which can be parceled out among individu-als . . . and *collective consumption goods* . . . which all enjoy in common in the sense that each individual's consumption of such a good leads to no subtraction from any other individual's consump-tion of that good.

This article is remarkable is many respects. For the purpose of understanding the concept of the tax state in modern public finance analysis, four aspects deserve attention. The first aspect is Samuelson's insistence on separating public finance into two wings, following the revenue and expenditure sides of the budget. Before this, public finance theorists tried to combine the revenue and expenditure aspects into one

The author should like to thank Richard A. Musgrave and Yuichi Shionoya for helpful comments.

single question.[1] Secondly, it is astonishing that the author of Wagner's Law devoted insufficient attention to determining a view on "optimal public expenditures." Thirdly, Samuelson is straightforward and honest in making it clear that his conceptualization of public finance is based on an *explicit assumption,* with no effort whatsoever to find an anchor in reality. Fourthly, an important omission slips into the second part of the first sentence, when optimal expenditures are contrasted, not with optimal revenues, but with taxation instead, introducing the presumption that taxes are the only, or at least the most important, source of revenue. These four aspects lie at the heart of Schumpeter's tax state analysis. The concept of the tax state serves to maintain a unified analysis of both revenues and expenditures. It tries to help us determine the institutional preconditions for particular fiscal policies. Thirdly, the concept of the tax state, as used by Schumpeter, tries to ground public financial analysis firmly into identifiable empirical circumstances. At the heart of the concept lies the distinction between different revenue sources, of which taxes are just one.

In stark contrast to Samuelson, Schumpeter used the concept of the tax state throughout his work, whenever he tried to focus on the politico-economic aspect of a particular problem—that is, on the interaction between economics and politics. The concept of the tax state does not belong to the realm of "pure theory," in the sense intended by Samuelson; rather, it is a central concept in Schumpeter's characteristic approach to political economy (*Sozialökonomik*) or public choice economics, as we might say today. The concept is clearly aimed at integrating aspects that tend to be dissociated when a "pure" economic approach is taken. This implies that the revenue and expenditure sides of the budget have to be analyzed simultaneously in the context of the political processes determining their levels and compositions. Secondly, the concept can be used to analyze the conditions that determine the extent of public sector activity; although Schumpeter (1970, 4–5) is careful in pointing out that an optimal policy cannot be determined in a scientific way. Central to the concept of the tax state is the distinction between different forms of revenues, taxes on the one hand, and various other nontax revenues on the other. Finally, the concept can only be fruitfully used if it is based on a thorough empirical foundation. When-

---

1. Of course, the Lindahl/Samuelson approach involves the simultaneous solution of supply and (virtual) demand, but the demand has no correspondence with the revenue side of a budget; nor does, incidentally, the supply side bear any resemblance with the expenditure side of an identifiable budget.

ever Schumpeter tried to invoke the concept, he provided this foundation, typically in terms of a historical narrative.

It should be clear from this short characterization of the concept of the tax state that it is not an easy one for the present-day economist to handle. Yet, as I shall try to argue in the remainder of this paper, if we look at Schumpeter's way of handling the concept, we cannot fail to be impressed, and perhaps even enticed to make use of it ourselves.

Among Schumpeter's numerous writings on public finance, his article on the tax state ("Die Krise des Steuerstaates," 1918) is certainly the most prominent. The article is the extended written version of a lecture held in Vienna in 1917. It appeared in German in 1918 for the first time and has been reprinted at least twice (Schumpeter 1918, 1953; Hickel 1976). In English, the article has been available since 1954 and it has recently been reprinted as well.[2] Perhaps because of its strange labeling as a contribution to "sociology," the paper seems to have been largely overlooked in the public finance literature. There is only one textbook that makes use of the concept (Wagner 1983, 245–47), and even Schumpeter's student and translator does not, although he cites the piece (Musgrave and Musgrave 1989, 126n.8). Most textbooks in public finance, including the two volumes of the *Handbook of Public Economics* (Auerbach and Feldstein 1985, 1987), have no reference to Schumpeter's public finance contributions whatsoever. When his name appears at all, other contributions of his are acknowledged.[3]

The scant attention Schumpeter's work in public finance receives today[4] could, of course, be a true reflection of its merits. A second possible reason for the lack of attention might be ignorance; if his work

---

2. The first translation by Wolfgang F. Stolper and Richard A. Musgrave appeared in 1954. The reprint can be found in Richard Swedburg 1991.

3. The only reference to Schumpeter in the *Handbook of Public Economics* is by Richard A. Musgrave, and acknowledges his *History of Economic Analysis* (1954a), with respect to his views on Ricardo. Joseph Stiglitz (1988, 71) acknowledges his theory of economic development and the importance of patents for the process of innovation.

4. There is no shortage of attention to Schumpeter's public finance work outside of mainstream public finance. The Marxist literature has always acknowledged his contribution (O'Connor 1973), which is also central to the new socioeconomic history (Berding 1981; Greve and Krüger 1982; von Witzleben 1985). Musgrave's (1992) own discussion of the subject sheds the most light on the question of why Schumpeter's contribution to public finance remains neglected. There is an unbridgeable intellectual (and at some times it appears also emotional) gap between Musgrave, the most effective author in postwar public finance, and his teacher, Schumpeter. According to Musgrave, Schumpeter fell victim to the "siren call of Hegelian diaiectics" (1992, 15) and "Goldscheid and Schumpeter were both too Wagnerian (or Hegelian) in their respective visions of fiscal crises. The *Götterdammerung* (sic) is not about to set in" (1992, 16).

is not part of the teaching of public finance, it is hardly surprising if no use is made of it.[5] Thirdly, the difficulty of integrating Schumpeter's concept of the tax state into standard public finance analysis could also account for the lack of doing so.

Whatever the reason may be, any of the three mentioned would warrant a reexamination of Schumpeter's tax state analysis. This is what I attempt in this essay. The essay has four parts in addition to this introduction. Part I indicates the context in which Schumpeter's tax state theory has to be placed. Part II explains the concept of the tax state as Schumpeter himself has introduced it in his own writings. Part III gives a number of examples of how Schumpeter used the concept for his own analytical purposes. These examples are taken, in part, from the German literature, and some of them have only recently become available. These examples clearly show what can be accomplished with the concept, and what it was not designed for. Finally, part IV indicates a number of current problems that might be usefully addressed in a Schumpeterian manner.

1. The Intellectual Context of Schumpeter's Tax State Theory

When public finance began to be taught as an academic discipline, the consensus was that taxes should only be used as a measure of last resort in order to generate revenues. von Wolff, who could conceive of taxes only in the sense of public prices for an identifiable service rendered by the state, nevertheless argued, in 1754, against their use, since the imposition of taxes would reduce the value of the object of taxation. He also cautioned against the use of contributions, one time assessments in cases of disaster and emergency. Similarly, he argued against the use of customs-duties, as they would raise the prices of basic necessities (Wolff 1754, 1057). Interestingly enough, Wolff does not even mention excise taxes, which had already become increasingly popular after glowing recommendations such as the one by Teutophilus (1685).[6]

---

5. This possibility is obviously irrelevant in the case of Musgrave's work. See also his *Leviathan Commeth—or Does He?* (1980).

6. It is perhaps worth our while to give the full information about the publication by Christian Teutophilus (Christian Tenzel 1685). The full title is: Entdeckte Gold-Grube in der Accise, Das ist, Kurzer, iedoch Gründlicher Bericht von der Accise, Dass dieselbe nicht allein die allerreicheste, sondern auch politeste, billigste, und nützlichste, ja eine gantz nötige collecte, und also Zwiefacher Ehren werth sey, Darinnen zur Genüge angeführet, Warum die Accise in Deutschland durchgehends, und auff was Arth dieselbe Anfangs in einer Provinz oder Stadt, in deren Nachbarschafft die Accise nicht, sondern die

An anonymously published report entitled "Confidential Letters About the Internal Situation of the Prussian Court Since the Death of Frederick II" (Anonymous 1807, 35) disapprovingly describes the efficiency of the Prussian revenue system, and then adds:

> A fourth of the revenues of the Prussian State is derived from the agricultural estates, and this is why I claim that not a single government in the world has more direct resources at its disposal than this one considering its size. None of the other civilized states is without public debt, and none can claim such a mass of land as Prussia.
>
> The public credit in Austria, France, Spain, England, Russia, Sweden, Denmark and Holland has as collateral not public lands, but simply an idea, the state guarantee, which is the basis of the public's confidence that the government will keep its promises. As this confidence increases or decreases, so increases or decreases also the value of the public bonds, to the disadvantage of both government and the governed. The government as a debtor is always dependent on the nation as a creditor. The nation measures its duty as a subject with the primitive value of money.[7]

In apparent contrast to this positive assessment, Adam Smith clearly disapproves of nontax revenues to the state, which he considers

---

contribution im schwange, einzuführen, In Sonderheit aber behauptet wird, dass dieselbe das rechte Fundament zu der neuesten Politik und Commercien-Beförderung lege, Wornebst auch comparative Von der Contribution und Schatzung etwas beygefüget ist, Allen Obrigkeiten zu grossen Auffnehmen, und populirung Ihres Landes, denen Staats- und Cammer-Bedienten, zur Verminderung Ihrer Geld-Sorge, und denen Unterthanen zur Erleichterung Ihrer Last Vorgestellet. See also Gustav Schmoller 1877 and Fritz Karl Mann [1937] 1978.

7. The source is: "Der preussische Staat zieht den vierten Theil seiner Revenuen aus den Domainen, dies veranlasst mich, zu behaupten: dass die Regierung mehr direkte Resourcen hat, wie irgend ein Staat in der Welt, das heisst, im Verhältnis zu seiner Grosse. Keiner der übrigens civilisierten Staaten ist schuldenfrei, und kann eine solche Masse von Grundeigenthum sein nennen, wie Preussen.

Die den Staatscredit in Östreich, Frankreich, Spanien, England, Russland, Schweden, Dännemark und Holland zu Grunde liegende Hypothek ist nicht einmal Grund und Boden, der Staatseigenthum wäre, sondern diese Hypothek beruht in der Regel nur auf einer Idee, (Staatsgarantie genannt) vermöge welcher man das Zutrauen zu der Regierung hervorbringt: sie werde stets Wort halten. Je nachdem dieses Zutrauen steigt oder fällt, je nachdem steigen und fallen auch die Staatspapiere und dieses Schwanken ist der Regierung so nachtheilig, wie den Regierten. Die Regerierung (als Schuldner) ist stets von dem Creditor (der Nation) dependent; und die Nation berechnet ihre Unterthänigkeitspflicht nach dem niedrigen Maaßstabe des Geldes" (Anonymous 1807, 35).

either inconsequential, in the case of entrepreneurial activities, or outright harmful, in the case of crown lands. To wit:

> Small republics have sometimes derived a considerable revenue from the profit of mercantile projects. The republic of Hamburg is said to do so from the profits of a public wine cellar and apothecary's shop. The state cannot be very great of which the sovereign has leisure to carry on the trade of a wine merchant or apothecary. (Smith 1776, V, II, I)

About the revenue from the management of agricultural states, Adam Smith has this to say:

> The revenue which, in any civilised monarchy, the crown derives from the crown lands, though it appears to cost nothing to individuals, in reality costs more to the society than perhaps any other equal revenue which the crown enjoys. It would, in all cases, be for the interest of the society to replace this revenue to the crown by some other equal revenue, and to divide the lands among the people, which could not well be done better perhaps, than by exposing them to public sale.
>   Lands for the purposes of pleasure and magnificence—parks, gardens, public walks, etc., possessions which are everywhere considered as causes of expense, not as sources of revenue—seem to be the only lands which, in a great and civilised monarchy ought to belong to the crown. (ibid.)

In contrast to Adam Smith, on the European continent a different school of thought exerted its influence.

The cameralists pushed actively for the establishment of manufacturing industries. Indeed, many leading cameralists, such as Johann Heinrich Gottlob von Justi (1717–71), perhaps the premier cameralist of them all, were not only university professors, but were also responsible for the conduct of such state enterprises as mines, glass works, and steel mills. In the event that these ventures failed, the cameralist advisors were held responsible, with their own careers often seriously endangered. With respect to the emphasis on the establishment of profitable enterprises, the difference between those countries that followed mercantilist policies and those that implemented the cameralist programs is striking. While earlier data are either incomplete or unreliable, there are relatively reliable data for the second half of the nineteenth century. These show the considerably greater extent to which the leading central European states, with huge military establishments, such as the Prussian kingdom, were able to finance their activities, predominantly from entrepreneurial ventures into activities such as agriculture and railroads.

For instance, Eheberg (1900) notes that for various dates in the early 1880s, net income from state agricultural enterprises comprised 1.5 percent of state revenues in France, 3 percent in England, 3.6 percent in Russia, and 3.9 percent in Austria-Hungary. The corresponding figure for Prussia was 16.4 percent. For roughly the same period, Rimpler (1900, 200) cites Adolf Wagner as finding that the net income from state agricultural enterprises provided 7.1 percent of state revenues in Baden, 9.7 percent in Saxony, 13.2 percent in Württemberg, and 17.3 percent in Bavaria. The same figures were only 4.1 percent in Switzerland, 3.6 percent in Greece, 3.4 percent in Russia, 3 percent in Italy, 2.9 percent in Denmark, 1.9 percent in the Netherlands, 1.4 percent in France, 1.2 percent in Norway, 1 percent in Belgium, 0.6 percent in England and Portugal, and 0.5 percent in Austria. Agricultural enterprises were, of course, steadily declining throughout the Western world as a source of state revenue. But some states, principally German, looked to the development of new enterprises to replace the declining agricultural revenues, while others did not, and looked to taxation instead. Railroads were of particular importance in this regard. According to Eheberg (1900), the share of state revenues produced by agricultural enterprises fell during the nineteenth century in Prussia from 26.7 percent in 1805 to 13.3 percent in 1850 to 3.2 percent in 1898–99. However, whereas the net income from railroads provided only 2.5 percent of Prussia's revenues in 1850, it provided 15.6 percent in 1861 and 43.6 percent in 1898–99.

For the budgetary year 1896–97, the net income from various Prussian state enterprises provided 56.8 percent of Prussia's revenues. State enterprises were likewise important sources of revenue in the other industrially advanced states in the federation. For instance, the comparable figures for 1896–97 were 59.5 percent for Saxony, 47.7 percent for Württemberg, and 30.7 percent for Bavaria (Eheberg 1900, 923). And even the newly formed empire (federation) itself, whose only enterprise was the postal service, was able to finance 5.6 percent of its budget from its lone enterprise. Finally, and to give an example where the concern for efficiency bears fruit only in the long run, net revenues from state forests by hectare in 1897 were (in marks) 42.91 in Württemberg, 41.42 in Baden, 26.5 in Alsace-Lorraine, and 15.99 in Saxony. By contrast, the equivalent figures were only 10.5 in France, 3.30 in Italy, 3.20 in Hungary, 1.72 in Spain, 1.68 in Austria, 0.48 in

Sweden, 0.41 in Norway, 0.20 in Russia, and 0.08 in Finland (Endres 1900, 1162).[8]

These figures show a fundamental difference between the economic style of a cameralist-inspired system and one based on the precepts of the great Scot. These differences have to be kept in mind as we try to understand Schumpeter's concept of the tax state. The cameralist state is part of the economy, whereas the Smithian state stands apart from the economy. In a cameralist system, the economy is partly public and partly private, but there are no substantial differences in the conduct of public or private enterprises. The Smithian economy is entirely private, and the economic activities that the state is still engaged in are not only minimal, they also follow completely different rules than if they were privately operated. As the example of the parks showed, in Smith's view, the operation of public production leads to nothing but expenses, not revenues. Schumpeter, in developing the concept of the tax state, obviously had the Smithian economic style in mind, not a cameralist one.[9]

In trying to locate Schumpeter's tax state approach in the history of thought on public finance, we have to be careful to distinguish it from other approaches that, on the surface, might seem similar. In particular, Wagner's Law could be construed as conveying a similar message. Let us therefore look carefully at what Wagner wrote in his first formulation of the "Law":

> On the whole, the realm of the state's activities has become ever more extensive, as the concept of the state developed, as people achieved higher and higher levels of civilization and culture, and the more demands were consequently addressed to the state. This has also led to a continuous increase in the required state revenues, an increase which was generally even higher relative to the

---

8. Furthermore, this conduct of the prince or state as businessman continued until the early twentieth century in Germany. For instance, Peter-Christian Witt (1970) reports that at the start of this century net revenues from public enterprises—which are to be distinguished from state monopolies—provided about one-third of the state budget.

9. The concept of *style* of economic conduct is a key notion that we owe to the historical school. It was used by Schmoller, Sombart, Spiethoff, and Schumpeter, who took style as a term of economic sociology. In order to understand and correctly interpret economic phenomena, one may want to look at the leading ideas and convictions (spirit) to which people subscribe and that will guide their actions; secondly at the techniques at their disposal; and thirdly at the organizational forms in which means and ends are combined or, alternatively, in which spirit and technique find their institutional realization.

Spiethoff actually gives five categories: i.e., the economic spirit, the natural and technical resources, the constitution of society, the constitution of the economy, and the economic process. For details, see Spiethoff 1933, 76–77.

increase of the extent of state activity. The cause for this relative difference lies in the means employed by the state: these have become ever more complex, comprehensive and costly as one and the same need required an ever more perfect, higher and refined way of being satisfied. Consider by way of example the educational system! The phenomenon has the character and importance of a "law" in political economy, the requirements of the state are constantly rising as people progress. (Wagner 1864; Umpfenbach 1859, 1860, I, II, B, I, 52)[10]

In relating public sector revenue needs to the stage of cultural development of people, Wagner also seems to take a "sociological" approach to public finance analysis, much as it was suggested that Schumpeter did. However, Wagner's Law (which also implies the Baumol-Bowen hypothesis) is difficult to pin down. As the stage of cultural development of people determines its needs vis-à-vis the state, the satisfaction of these needs is the prime agent of cultural development. The line of causation goes both ways, and there seems to be no limit. Trying to establish a limit, on the other hand, is the most important purpose of Schumpeter's tax state analysis. Another difference is crucial—many other less crucial ones will be mentioned later. In placing Wagner between Smith and the Cameralists, we find him squarely on the side of the Cameralists, as he, too, emphasized nontax revenues over and above tax revenues. Wagner's Law does not at all establish an ever-increasing need for tax revenues; rather, it sees public entrepreneurship as one of the most important agents of cultural and economic

---

10. The original German text reads:

Im ganzen ist der Bereich der Staatsthätigkeit immer ausgedehnter geworden, je mehr sich die Staatsidee entwickelte, eine je höhere Stufe der Civilisation und Cultur ein Volk erreichte, je mehr neue Anforderungen in Folge dessen an den Staat gestellt wurden. Damit ist dann aber auch die Grösse des Staatsbedarfes fortwährend gewachsen, und zwar relativ meist noch stärker als der Bereich der Staatsthätigkeit, weil das System der zur Erreichung der Staatszwecke dienenden Mittel complizirter, umfassender, kostspieliger wurde und ein und dasselbe Bedürfnis auf eine immer vollkommenere, höheren, feinere Weise seine Befriedigung verlangte. Welcher Fortschritt ist z.B. in dieser Beziehung im Unterrichtswesen eingetreten! Die Erscheinung hat den Charakter und die Bedeutung eines "Gesetzes" im Leben des Staates: der Staatsbedarf ist bei forschreitenden Völkern in regelmässiger Vermehrung begriffen. Hiermit steht die bekannte Richtung der gegenwärtigen Zeit auch keineswegs in Widerspruch, wonach gerade jetzt in einer Menge von Lebensbeziehungen der Staatsbürger, besonders in der speciell volkswirthschaftlichen Sphäre, die befördernde, bevormundende, regulierende, in Alles sich einmischende Thätigkeit der Staatsgewalt wenigstens bei den germanischen Nationen vielfach beschränkt und beseitigt wird.

development. Schumpeter, on the other hand, stands in Smith's tradition. He uses his tax state analysis, among other methods, to refute the need for a recapitalization of the (Austrian) state, a suggestion made by Rudolf Goldscheid (1917). It was Goldscheid's book that prompted Schumpeter's first essay.[11]

In proposing his tax state analysis, Schumpeter could build on yet another theoretical approach, linking public sector revenue analysis with an economic theory of the state. This was the contribution of the Swedish School, and, notably, Knut Wicksell's new principle of just taxation (Wicksell 1896). Pareto, in his *Mind and Society* (1935, IV § 2271), had criticized attempts by the Austrians, notably Emil Sax, to apply the marginal utility principle to public sector analysis. Pareto comments as follows:

> Noteworthy among such derivations is a pseudo-scientific variety, obtained by extending the notions of pure economics to the social "needs" of a people. It is assumed that "needs" are satisfied by "the State"; then, by considerations of marginal utilities, one derives the norms of a certain equilibrium between "needs" and the "sacrifices" required by satisfying them. So one gets theories that conform to formal logic in certain cases, but which are so far removed from reality as at times to have nothing in common with them.

Likewise, Wicksell criticized Sax for "not taking proper account of the fact that for the evaluation which the economist must insist on, of the diverse public needs in real public affairs, the requisite agency and necessary institutions are lacking" (Wicksell 1896, 89).[12]

Taking this into account, Wicksell set out to describe such a set of institutions on the basis of a specific model of public decision making. In doing so, he started from the assumption that the only possible way of assessing public needs must be on the basis of individual evaluations. In order to ensure that it was on the basis of these individual evaluations that public decisions on the budget were made, he postulated that these decisions should require, as they do in the marketplace, the voluntary consent of those who were to face the burden of any particular tax. That is: he wanted the tax to be a voluntary contribution on the part of the taxpayer, to be a price instead of a tax. This is the Wicksellian principle of voluntary exchange in the public sector, and from this principle he

---

11. On this debate see also Backhaus 1989.

12. My translation. This part of the essay was not translated for the 1958 English edition.

deduced, under the peculiar institutional circumstances of his time, procedural implications.

This distinction between the principle itself and the procedural implications is important, because ignorance of this distinction has always given rise to objections to the effect that Wicksell's model was impracti-
· cal. However, the main purpose of Wicksell's article was to propose, as he makes clear in the title of his article, "A New Principle of Just Taxation"; the procedure that he proposed in order to implement this principle is to be distinguished from the principle itself, since the procedure represents nothing more than Wicksell's effort to show that his was more than lofty armchair speculation, an objection to which he was very sensitive, and that is therefore recurrently dealt with in the text.

Wicksell's principle, in itself, is, as Hennipman has pointed out in detail (Hennipman 1980, 1982), precisely the same principle that later was to bear Pareto's name. This principle is not a decision rule,[13] but an equilibrium condition instead. When this condition is met, a state can be said to be optimal in a certain well-defined sense.[14] It is important to note that a Wicksellian or Paretian equilibrating move also implies a consensual decision. Put differently, a Wicksellian or Paretian equilibrium or optimum defines a point where the potential for further consensual decisions has been exhausted, at least for the time being.

In order to design an institution that would generate solutions without satisfying his principle, Wicksell made the assumption that the Swedish people consisted of several homogeneous groups (classes) all of which could find adequate representation in Parliament according to their relative importance and size.[15]

This parliament was supposed to be confronted with the government of the Crown, which, while not being immediately responsible to the people, was supposed to follow mainly dynastic ends and conduct economic enterprises in the interest of the Crown's purse (Wicksell, 1958, 86).[16] For this reason, the Crown was supposed to have a natural interest in expanding the scope of public activities—a disposition of interests that, according to Wicksell, accounted for much of Wagner's "Law."

---

13. Although some people think that it is. See, e.g., Leibenstein (1962), who states that the "Pareto choice rule" gives a veto power to each individual.

14. On the distinction between the equilibrium condition and the rule of unanimity, see Hennipman (1980); on the Pareto Principle see Backhaus 1980, 1981.

15. In his later discussions, he used "class" and "political party" synonymously (p. 114 in the German original). In the translation, this is not apparent, since (p. 90) "Partei oder (or) Volksclasse" was translated as "parties and (!) social classes."

16. P. 108 in the German original.

In this bargaining situation between Parliament and the Crown, the Crown was the supplier of a public good or service, the price of which was to be determined by its cost and to be borne by the tax payer, while the quantity was subject to negotiation between Parliament and the Crown. Since society was assumed to be heterogeneous, the ever-eager interest in increasing the scope of public activities, on the one hand, and · changing majorities in Parliament, on the other, would give rise to an almost infinite expansion of the public sector, far beyond the optimum characterized by Wicksell's principle. For this reason, Wicksell proposed the requirement of relative unanimity (approval of some three-quarters or nine-tenths of the vote cast in Parliament) in budgetary decisions, subject to various qualifications. Also, each decision to spend was tied to another decision, taken simultaneously, on the distribution of the tax burden.

This is, however, not the entire proposal. The proposal, as was pointed out above, rested on the proposition that taxes should be tax prices and, for that matter, voluntary contributions. Since the Crown was supposed to have a tendency to continuously increase its realm of activity, each class (or party in Parliament) was to be entitled to withhold taxes after giving due notice (Wicksell 1958, 94).[17]

The procedure was to be rather complex, involving an earmarking of taxes and the necessity of specifying precisely which tax was to be withheld. As soon as a particular party (social class) withheld its share of the tax(es) for a particular good or service, the remaining groups in Parliament could decide upon a new distribution of the burden of taxation, which was then, again, subject to (relatively) unanimous approval. Obviously, the withholding party was not likely to object to any new proposal that did not involve any tax share of their own. However, threatening to withhold taxes carried the danger that the production of the good or the service might be cut back, or even discontinued. For this reason, Wicksell was confident that strategic behavior and abuse of the veto power was likely to be rare (Wicksell 1958, 104).[18]

Moreover, Wicksell took a very strict position, insofar as lack of (near-) unanimity of approval was concerned. Private initiative, in his view, was always an alternative to public provision (Wicksell 1958, 89).[19]

Finally, it seems to be worthwhile to consider an exception to the principle of relatively unanimous consent in Parliament that Wicksell made. Since even with institutional reform, no parliament can start from

---

17. P. 120 in the German original.
18. P. 157 in the German original.
19. P. 112 in the German original.

scratch, some expenditures simply have to be made, because the State has earlier incurred obligations to do so.

Into this category, Wicksell placed certain compensations to be paid, upon discontinuance of services; but also the public debt. Since the public debt has to be serviced in some way, some decision invariably has to be made as to how the tax burden is to be shared among the different classes in society. For this reason, the majority rule was to be followed in those cases in which a budgetary decision positively had to be made.

Schumpeter's approach shares with Wicksell's the historical foundation, the attempt at integrating public sector economics and the economic theory of politics, and the insistence on simultaneously considering revenues and expenditures. The two approaches are different, in that Schumpeter does not derive a constitutional principle that can be implemented according to economic and political circumstances of time and place; more importantly, Schumpeter is much more radical in applying the Italian tradition to public finance for his analytical purposes. As with Pareto, when it comes to public sector decision making, Schumpeter emphasizes redistribution over allocation. The overriding feature of the tax state, in Schumpeter's analysis, is the sheer force of taxing power, not a consensual process between political authorities and taxpayers.

The proceeding survey allows us to place Schumpeter within the history of thought on public finance in a tradition that emphasizes the particular style of an economy and the conduct of the state within and toward this economy. The style determines the constraints under which economic agents operate, and under which the public sector authorities can achieve their objectives, by different means. Crucial for our purposes is the importance of taxation as a source for generating public revenues. When taxes play a relatively minor role as sources of public revenues, or when they are essentially tax prices, as in the early concepts (Wolff) or under Wicksell's principle, then public sector revenue seeking will place few or no burdens on economic activity. Under these circumstances, the role of the state faces no inherent constraint. When, on the other hand, taxes are forced payments wrought from economic agents, the impact on scope and extent of private economic activity can be large. It is this economic style on which Schumpeter focused.

2. Schumpeter's Concept of the Tax State

In his introduction to the collection of essays by Schumpeter, Richard Swedberg equates Schumpeter's tax state with the "capitalist state" (1991, 74). This characterization misses a crucial aspect of Schumpeter's approach. The concept of the tax state is clearly related to Sombart's "modern capitalist system" (Sombart 1927, 1933; Schumpeter 1927), but it is not the same: rather, it is its complement. The tax state and the capitalist economic system are two systems that exist side by side, mutally supporting and determining each other's mode of operation, while these modes of operation are completely different. The difference, in Schumpeter's view, is so big that the standard economic tools that have been developed for the analysis of market exchange are not readily applicable for analyzing the economic consequences of taxation. These consequences can be so variegated as to mitigate an accurate understanding of the extent and scope of the influence. The influence of particular taxes extends well beyond short-run quantity and quality effects. The impact depends upon circumstances of time and place, but, even more importantly, on the accumulated process of individual reactions, which can form entirely different patterns. The analysis of the consequences of taxation, therefore, has to be one that not only takes a long-run perspective, and thereby can capture accumulated and self-reinforcing structural effects, but it also must go beyond the partial microeconomic analysis we owe to Marshall. The standard microanalysis has to be complemented by a macroanalysis that is partly standard economic, partly politico-economic, and, by virtue of its integration of different aspects, an approach sui generis. This general characterization I should like to base on a sequence of quotes from Schumpeter's essay, that will allow the reader to capture the main features of Schumpeter's tax state approach better than any other way. About the method itself, he says:

> The full fruitfulness of this approach is seen particularly at those turning points, or better epochs, during which existing forms begin to die off and to change into something new, and which always involve a crisis of the old fiscal methods. This is true, both of the causal importance of fiscal policy (insofar as fiscal events are an important element in the causation of all change) and of the symptomatic significance (insofar as everything that happens has its fiscal reflection). Notwithstanding all the qualifications which always have to be made in such a case, we may surely speak of a special set of facts, a special set of problems, and of a special approach—in short, of a special field: fiscal sociology, of which much may be expected.
>
> Of these approaches, the development of which lies as yet in the lap of the gods, there is one which is of particular interest to us: the view of the state, of its nature, its forms, its fate, as seen from the fiscal side. The word "tax state" is a child of this view, and the

following investigations are concerned with the implications quite clearly contained in this term. (1992, 101–2)

The analysis then has to be invoked at the turning points, and it is not concerned with small movements, but with design (form), internal processes, and future performance (fate). The facts required for this type of analysis are singular, not contained in the general statistics that require system stability to be usefully collected at all.

Historically, the states granted the princes taxes in order to finance a common purpose. This, in Schumpeter's view, facilitated the development of the state as such: the princes (as was the case under the cameralist regimes) were public entrepreneurs who controlled countries. The state becomes an entity apart from such entrepreneurs, and, in this sense, the tax as an institution is constitutive for the emergence of states. But, on the other hand, the tax-financed state also helps in the development of the economic system that has to support the taxing state. He writes:

> Taxes not only helped to create the state. They helped to form it. The tax system was the organ the development of which entailed the other organs. Tax bill in hand, the state penetrated the private economies and won increasing dominion over them. The tax brings money and calculating spirit into corners in which they do not dwell as yet, and thus becomes a formative factor in the very organism which has developed it. (1992, 108)

The interdependence between economy and tax state goes even further. To the extent that the state can finance its needs through taxation, which requires a supportive economic system, this instrument of revenue collecting will shape the state itself. Today, we call this phenomenon "rent seeking." Schumpeter writes:

> The kind and level of taxes are determined by the social structure, but once taxes exist they become a handle, as it were, which social powers can grip in order to change this structure. However, the whole fruitfulness of this approach can here only be hinted at. (Schumpeter 1992, 108)

The duality of the nature of the economy, on the one hand, and the tax state, on the other, by the way, also leads Schumpeter to the prediction, since proven true, that states that try, at the same time, to be the economic system, will collapse—i.e., that one organization acting as both the economic organization and the political organization is an impossibility. Nor can state socialism exist, nor can the tax state exist, if people follow social purposes in their daily lives, instead of their own:

> Only where individual life carries its own center of gravity within itself, where its meaning lies in the individual and his personal sphere, where the fulfillment of the personality is its own end, only then can the state exist as a real phenomenon. (1992, 109)

The reason for this definition of the preconditions of the tax state is fairly straightforward, and Schumpeter develops it further on. The tax can only be extracted from a consumer's or producer's rent. The tax can only appropriate a part of the rent, since otherwise, without the remaining rent, the activity undertaken in order to reap the rent would simply cease. But this is the same as saying that the individual and the public purpose have to be diametrically opposed. Or as he puts it:

> It is part of its nature that it opposes individual egotism as a representative of the common purpose. Only then is it a separate, distinguishable social entity. (1992, 110)

In general, when we proceed with the analysis of a particular tax, we invoke the ceterus paribus assumption, as far as the structure of the economy onto which the tax is being levied is concerned. If a tax on a particular product is being introduced, we will generally leave the demand and supply curves intact and derive the result as we move along the curves, basing the incidence analysis on elasticities of existing demand and supply curves. Schumpeter, however, with his tax state analysis tries to reach beyond this partial approach. He insists that the tax state also deeply affects the structure of the economy, which implies that the shape of the demand and supply curves will be affected. To wit:

> It goes without saying that there is more to the state than the collection of taxes necessitated by the common need that was their origin. Once the state exists as reality and as a social institution, once it has become the center of the persons who man the governmental machine and whose interests are focused upon it, finally, once the state is recognized as suitable for many things even by those individuals whom it confronts—once all this has happened, the state develops further and soon turns into something the nature of which can no longer be understood merely from the fiscal stand-

point, and for which the finances become a serving tool. If the finances have created and partly formed the modern state, so now the state on its part forms them and enlarges them—deep into the flesh of the private economy. (1992, 110–11)

Having emphasized the power of the tax state in molding the private economy, it is natural that Schumpeter next focuses on the limits of the tax state. Here, the method he needs to use becomes particularly clear. Tax state analyses require a case study approach, since general theories of taxation need to assume as constant what needs to be analyzed as variable:

In any case, the state has its definite limits. These are, of course, not conceptually definable limits of its field of social action, but limits to its fiscal potential. These vary considerably in each specific case according to the wealth or poverty of the country, to the concrete details of its national and social structure, and to the nature of its wealth. There is a great difference between new, active, and growing wealth and old wealth, between entrepreneurial and rentier states. The limits of their fiscal potential may also differ according to the extent of military expenses or the debt service, to the power and morality of its bureaucracy, and to the intensity of the "state-consciousness" of its people. But they are always there and they may be theoretically determined in general terms from the nature of the state. (1992, 111)

The strictest limit, however, arises from the antinomy between state and economy. As Yin and Yang in Chinese philosophy, in Schumpeter's conception, the tax state and the modern capitalist system as described by Sombart mutually exclude and at the same time complement each other. One is driven by active entrepreneurship, the other by passive routine; one lives off the other, but both need each other and are shaped by each other:

Everywhere, the tax state (J. B.) confronts the private economies with relatively few means—private economies whose meaning and drive are service for the private sphere and which produce only for the latter—while the state is dependent on what it can wring from them. Though the state may be felt everywhere, and notwithstanding the phraseologies hammered into the citizens by its organs from their childhood, it remains something peripheral, something alien to the proper purpose of the private economy, even something hostile, in any case something derived. (1992, 111–12)

Having adopted this dialectical approach, it is not surprising that Schumpeter had a keen understanding of what later became known as the Laffer-curve. The relationship between tax yield and tax rate, which can be exploited as political success when tax rates go down and tax yields go up, is illustrated with reference to Pitt and Gladstone. But again, the treatment is much more complex than Arthur Laffer's was. Firstly, as Wagner did, but with an opposite implication, Schumpeter relates the tax state and the level of cultural development. Secondly, he rejects the standard tax incidence analysis as being too incomplete. And thirdly, he questions the very possibility of drawing Arthur Laffer's curve, as it may be too difficult to define the most relevant dimensions. To wit:

> In this world the state lives as an economic parasite. It can withdraw from the private economy only as much as is consistent with the continued existence of this individual interest in every particular socio-physiological situation. In other words, the tax state must not demand from the people so much, that they lose financial interest in production or at any rate cease to use their best energies for it. . . . However, though the limits are nearer or farther away in different situations, they are nevertheless in every case recognizable on the basis of our principle. Let us consider first how much indirect taxes can contribute. The effects which emanate from them through the process of shifting and of curtailment of consumption cannot be described briefly in their enormous complexity. However, we are not interested in the manner in which, retarding and destroying, they affect first the economy, then the way of life, and then finally the cultural level. Nor are we interested in investigating the extent to which the low intellectual and moral level of the majority of the population in most countries today can in the final analysis be traced back to these effects. . . . The determination of that level which yields the maximum revenue meets with two great practical difficulties. There is first the fact that every significant indirect tax enforces technical and commercial changes in the productive apparatus, the consequences of which are the most difficult to follow. Second, there is the difficulty that the situation in which the tax was imposed does not remain unchanged in other respects; there are practically always other "disturbances" which may weaken the effect of a tax on the consumer . . . or which accentuate the effect of the tax on the consumer and dampen it for the producer. (1992, 112–13)

So far, the quotes seem to indicate that Schumpeter's treatment defies standard economic analysis, as he is constantly broadening the realm of problems, effects, and intervening variables beyond our ability to handle all of this simultaneously. Perhaps it was this feeling that slapped the term fiscal sociology onto his work at the time when "sociological" could no longer be called a recommendation when used by economists. This was, of course, different when Schumpeter used the term. In his time, leading economists such as Max Weber, Werner Sombart, or Vilfredo Pareto were creating sociology not least for the purpose of creating the proper scientific environment in which the further pursuit and refinement of economic analysis and methods made sense and could be considered productive.

This general characterization also applies to Schumpeter's use of his "sociological" tax state approach. Perhaps nowhere as clearly as in his treatment of direct taxes do we see how radical his approach is to applying economic theory in public finance analysis. His treatment of income taxes, which clearly builds on Schmoller's "*Lehre vom Einkommen in ihrem Zusammenhang mit den Grundprinzipien der Steuerlehre*" (1863), differentiates economically between the different types of income, entrepreneurial profit, monopoly profit, interest, rent, and wages, and then considers, in turn, the impact of income taxes on each of these. He is well aware that, from an administrative point of view, it will be next to impossible to implement the requisite policy conclusions, as they are almost diametrically opposed between one category and the other.[20] It is this impossibility of observing the theoretically distinguishable magnitudes that prompts Schumpeter to go beyond economics and to consider the politico-economic interdependencies. As a tax administration cannot distinguish between incomes that economic theory tells us are different, but does not teach us to differentiate unmistakably, every income tax will have multiple consequences that differ from one subject of taxation to the next. However careful we may be in designing the tax structure in such a way as to ensure a containment of its destructive effects, we will still fail or, in Schumpeter's characteristically figurative language:

> In all these cases we have ideal tax objects, provided one can always recognize them beyond doubt, separate them from others which look similar but are very different, and provided that a correct tax technique for their treatment can be devised. This has never been done successfully so far. In practice we mostly find something like an attempt to load a sack of flour on the shadow of an ass. (1992, 114–15)

---

20. Schumpeter is also keenly aware of the administrative techniques of taxation. See Schumpeter (1985c, 77–83).

In distinguishing between ideal objects of taxation and those forms of income that should not be taxed, the first important difference is between taxes on income and taxes that actually require the cession of property. The latter can obviously only be a measure of last resort, resorted to in times of desperation. Schumpeter, as Minister of Finance, proposed such a measure in order to deal with the war debt and stabilize the currency. Secondly, Schumpeter considers enterpreneurial profits proper and writes:

> Entrepreneurial profit proper—as distinct from interest with which it used to be combined, from the risk premium which obviously is no net income, and from the wages of the entrepreneur which is a special case of wages—arises in the capitalist economy wherever a new method of production, a new commercial combination, or a new form or organization is successfully introduced. It is the premium which capitalism attaches to innovation. As it arises continuously so it disappears continuously through the effect of competition which, baited by the profit, follows up immediately on the innovator. . . . We are not here concerned with the obvious consequences for the economy and thus in the last analysis also for the finances of the state. Only one thing is important for us: that there is a limit to the taxation of entrepreneurial profit beyond which tax pressure cannot go without first damaging and then destroying the tax object. An ideally perfect tax practice which would give individual treatment to each individual case of entrepreneurial profit as it arises, could collect much higher sums than the actual practice which in spite of relatively small success nevertheless brutally destroys many possibilities for economic development. (1992, 113–14)

As proper objects of taxation, Schumpeter identifies monopoly profits and the ground rent. Monopolies, of course, have a long history of being used as substitutes for taxation when run by the state. On the ground rent, Henry George built his proposal for progress and prosperity. Yet, again, Schumpeter is cautious. In establishing the magnitude of the ground rent, interest on the purchase price must be deducted. Similarly, windfall profits can be taxed, yet:

> Though most of the time it is very difficult to single out among the mass of phenomena which the layman calls an unearned increase in value, those cases to which the epithet really applies, in particular those in which the increase in value does not fulfill the function of a risk premium or of an interest element. (1992, 114)

Similarly, the remainder of the analysis proceeds.[21] Again and again, the warning of the limits of the tax state recurs, which follows from the complementary relationship between the tax state, on the one hand, and the capitalist economy, on the other:

> And additional taxation of higher labor incomes, which are the only ones, which matter in practice, discourages all above-average effort wherever the effort is not its own end. Again, the economic effects of these taxes do not interest us here. What matters to us is that the possible tax yield is limited not only by the size of the taxable object less the subsistence minimum of the taxable subject, but also by the nature of the driving forces of the free economy. (1992, 115)

In order to illustrate the distortionary effects of taxation, public finance textbooks tend to invoke the lump sum tax as a benchmark case. The lump sum tax is an analytical construct with no counterpart in reality for the single purpose of demonstrating the distortionary effects of taxes measured as the difference between levying a lump sum tax and levying any particular tax under consideration. Schumpeter also introduces a benchmark case, but his is an imaginary object of taxation that may have some counterpart in reality. Again, the language is colorful:

> The case of the childless millionaire living off his inherited rents, whose income is given once and for all and can therefore be taxed without fear of diminution, this case is rare, though the time may come when the whole bourgeoisie will be nothing but a childless rentier-millionaire. (1992, 115)

3. Applications

Schumpeter used the concept of the tax state, which he had developed in his 1917 article, throughout the remainder of his scholarly career. This is particularly true for his writings in theoretical and applied public finance, most of which have not been published in English.[22] In his *On Money,* the distinction between the state as a producer (the entrepreneurial state) and the tax state again becomes crucial (Schumpeter 1970, 136).

---

21. See also his stimulating article on the income tax (Schumpeter 1985b).

22. See, in particular, the two volumes edited by Wolfgang F. Stolper and Christian Seidl: *Aufsätze zur Wirtschaftspolitik* (Schumpeter 1985a) and *Politsche Reden* (Schumpeter 1992).

Again, in his *Business Cycles* (1939), there is an extensive tax state analysis (chap. 8). As compared to the 1917 article, Schumpeter has even hardened his critique of standard public finance theory and reinforced his insistence that the causes and consequences of taxation can only be adequately understood when political and economic factors are simultaneously taken into account. The following quote shows to what extent Schumpeter has been consistent in this respect:

> There is (comparative) agreement about the effects of indirect taxes, such as specific taxes on the quantity produced or sold of a commodity. This agreement we owe to a fairly well elaborated theory which, though antiquated, is still widely accepted by economists and has recently been somewhat improved by borrowings from the theories of imperfect competition, of expectation, and so on. Its assumptions, however, limit its results to the case of small taxes and/or individual commodities of small importance. The technical reason for this has an important counterpart in real life: wherever taxes are so small as to be amendable to analytical treatment by the calculus, they are also too small to affect the fundamental contours of economic behavior as reflected in the budgets of firms and housholds and, hence, do interfere significantly with economic processes in general and the cyclical process of evolution and its permanent results in particular. . . . Most taxes which are not small in that wider sense, on the one hand cannot be handled by that method—further repercussions, more fundamental changes in the economic system, reactions from and through the sphere of money and credit must be then taken into account—and on the other hand, to interfere with the results of business processes, *e.g.,* with the steady rise in the standard of living of the masses *as far as it is due to the working of the capitalist machine.*
>
> This, however, marks the point at which disagreement begins. The fiscal problem of our time does not primarily consist in the amount of income required by the modern state, but in the fact that, owing to the moral valuations prevailing, that amount must also be raised by heavy taxes and, moreover, by heavy taxes framed not only without a view to a minimum disturbance but regardless of disturbance, and in some cases even with a view to maximizing it. (Schumpeter 1939, VIII, C)

Similarly, his position on direct taxes remains unchanged, just further elaborated with respect to the problem of cyclical developments. On inheritance taxes he writes:

As in that special form of the profit motive which is embodied in the term *family position* and is largely eliminated by inheritance taxes of the modern type, it is as reasonable to hope that high inheritance taxes, being taxes on "static" wealth, will not affect industrial "progress," *i.e.* the creation of new wealth, as it would be to hope that a prohibitive railroad fare will not affect traffic if passengers be allowed to board the train free of charge and the fare be collected from them after they have taken their seats. (Schumpeter 1939, VIII, C)

The last quote not only documents Schumpeter's unabated good humor, but, more importantly, his quest for a dynamic economic theory. In this quest, the concept of the tax state plays a pivotal role.

Schumpeter has used the concept of the tax state in so many different contexts that it seems to be as impossible as it would be boring to give a complete list of the applications. In showing what Schumpeter could do with the theoretical instrument that he forged for himself, I shall discuss only two examples, examples that are noteworthy because they allowed him to arrive at a specific and concrete answer to a political problem that he confronted. The first example is the one that prompted his essay on the tax state. Goldscheid had proposed to recapitalize the exhausted state by expropriating profitable industries and allowing the state to use these profits as revenues. Having taken such great pains to show the limits of the tax state, one should expect that Schumpeter might welcome this proposal. Yet the opposite is true. His answer comes in two parts. The first part deals with an estimate of the difference between raising direct and indirect taxes and expropriating the same companies. This part of the argument is based on his theory of income taxation, which has already been outlined above. Schumpeter excludes the expropriation of monopolies as a different case and proceeds with the comparative analysis of the yield of a corporate income tax raised from a competitive corporation and the possible yield of operating that same corporation by the state. He writes:

The decisive criterion is whether, apart from any monopoly position, which it might secure for itself, the state does or does not continue to work within the framework of a free economy whose data and methods it has to accept in its own enterprises. If it does and thus works in a capitalist spirit toward as high a money profit as possible, then its possible profits are limited by the economic laws of capitalist production. And these limits are narrower than the layman believes. Since the state must work with money capital just as any other entrepreneur, and since it can raise this money only through loans, it is unlikely that the remaining profit will be much larger than what could have been extracted from the same industry by direct and indirect taxation including taxes on the income of this industry. This is likely to be true even with extreme fiscal exploitation of a possible monopoly position and even if we disregard the small entrepreneurial ability which the state in fact has. (Schumpeter 1991, 116)

It is important to note that this argument does not exclude expropriating ground rent, and, thus, does not completely refute Goldscheid's proposal. It was therefore completely compatible for Schumpeter to, on the one hand, reject the socialization of competitive corporations and, on the other, take a seat on the German socialization commission that was charged with determining the feasibility of socializing (parts of) the mining industry.

Secondly, it is clear that Schumpeter assumes that the Austrian state, about which he is writing, will not earn entrepreneurial profits. This judgment largely conforms to the historical record.

The dynamic aspect of Schumpeter's argument focuses on the process of reintegrating the Austrian economy into the world economy. Again, the language is vivid. He turns Goldscheid's proposal on its head and emphasizes the material transfer of goods (for example, the acquisition of resources from abroad), instead of the legal transfer of ownership titles. To wit:

The second task of recapitalization consists of arranging for the supply of those goods, particularly raw materials, which have to come from abroad. It is frequently said that the private economies will be unable to procure the necessary supplies and for this reason we have to go beyond the essential nature of the tax state. Anyone who has the slightest idea about these things knows that any good bank has better access to foreign credits and will be accommodated much more readily abroad than the state. In the difficult postwar situation with its struggle for raw materials, it is clearly just that business ingenuity which in our as yet "capitalistically diseased" world is set in motion by the prospect of large private gain, that will be able to find ways and means here and there to wrest one or the other shipload out of the hand of stronger purchasing power and make it available to Austria. . . . It is, of course, certain that in the process we will not get the distribution of raw materials which anyone considers ideal and that many entrepreneurs may need government subsidies; but it is equally certain that this is of no importance at the time in which the real question is to get anything at all of those goods that we need most. The wage level and the amount of liquid working capital will ensure that these essential imports will be the most profitable from the standpoint of the private economy. Let them insist that an ideally functioning state could perform better. This it is idle to discuss. It is certain that a private economy can *also* do it, and do it quickly and promptly if the bureaucracy does not get in its way and piles up a mountain of paper between us and the necessary raw materials. (1991, 129–30)

Although Schumpeter's tax article is not an apolitical piece, and it may even have led to his later appointment as the first Minister of Finance of the Austrian Republic, it was still written as a scholarly contribution to an ongoing debate about the future economic system of postwar Austria. Schumpeter, however, also relied on his tax state theoretical approach in his political speeches and interviews, when he actually had to solve the political problems that he had earlier reflected upon in academic solitude. *The ultimate test of a method lies in its application, and we can judge from Schumpeter's own choice of analytical methods, in time of action, how he appreciated them.*

Schumpeter's position in the newly formed (revolutionary) government was a peculiar one. The constitution of the newly formed German remainder of Austria, the official name of which was actually "German-Austria," called for the unification of this country with Germany. This was also the official cabinet position, but Schumpeter favored, instead, a loose confederation of the successor states of the Austrian empire in a Danube trade zone. With this plan, Schumpeter tried to save the economic part of the old Austrian-Hungarian empire, as the corresponding state had vanished as a consequence of World War I. Since we have already seen that Schumpeter considered the state and the economy as complementary to one other, the political purpose of his proposal is immediately apparent. The unification of Austria and Germany was, of course, opposed by the victorious powers in Versailles and Saint-Germain, implying that Schumpeter's minority position was extremely difficult to maintain during the acrimonious tug of war about the peace conditions. The second important issue in the peace negotiations was the insistence on reparation payments by the victorious powers, an issue which had prompted Keynes to resign from the staff of the British delegation. In the eyes of his cabinet colleagues, Schumpeter had complicated the Austrian government's position by painting what they considered a rosy picture of Austria's postwar finances. In fact, his position was sim-

ply that, provided that the Danube federation could go through and that
the question of the debt of the perished Austrian state could be solved
by persisting as well, the Austrian economy would be able to maintain
an Austrian (tax) state. These two conditions were at stake politically.
When it became apparent that neither of them would be met, that
Austria could not be part of a larger market nor rid itself of the outstanding debt of its legal predecessor and, in addition would face large reparation demands, Schumpeter, again relying on his tax state analysis,
pointed out, in sometimes dramatic speeches, the impossibility of what
was being requested.[23]

The analytical stucture of Schumpeter's speeches and interviews is
exactly the same as the analytical structure of his articles. When he
discusses the possibilities of servicing the war debt, he analyzes the yield
of the different economic income streams one by one, in this case on an
aggregate level. He then tries to determine the relative magnitudes and,
in comparing them with the demands, draws the conclusion that what is
being politically demanded is an economic impossibility and, therefore,
will not happen in the long run. He argues similarly when he deals with
the Danube federation. If a country is so small that its market will be of
a suboptimal size, it must enter a customs union as a matter of economic
necessity. Schumpeter was well aware of the long time horizon needed
for history to run its course. He was also aware of the different stages on
which the politico-economic drama would be played out. Speaking
about the ultimate necessity of the Danube customs federation, he told a
Viennese newspaper:

> Nobody questions the political sovereignty of these successor states,
> but to erect customs barriers arounnd six or ten million people is
> not only a mistake, not only a crime, but above all it is ridiculous.[24]

Perhaps it was Schumpeter's tragedy as a politician that, although his
analysis was right, as a Minister of Finance, he was politically and
socially proven wrong. He had to act on three stages simultaneously;
on the academic stage, the political stage, and the social stage. Ultimately, more than half a century and several catastrophes later, his
economic analysis has been proven right. Yet, when he had to combine
his political economic insight with political ambition and social apti-

23. See, in particular, parts III and IV of his *Politische Reden* (Schumpeter 1992).

24. "Niemand bezweifelt die politischen Selbständigkeiten dieser Teilstaaten, aber
wirtschaftliche Zollgebiete zu errichten, die sich um sechs oder zehn Millionen Einwohner
schliessen, ist nicht nur ein Fehler, nicht nur ein Verbrechen, sondern vor allem einen
Lächerlichkeit" (Schumpeter 1992, 103–4).

tude, he ended up being considered burned out as an economist and scholar,[25] ridiculed as a politician, and even threatened with indictment over the sale of a mining company he apparently could not prevent from being sold. These three stages of scholarly correctness, crime, and ridicule, which he had alluded to, all related to the three stages of his own fate in a dramatic way.

4. Conclusion: The Tax State as an Analytical Concept

Schumpeter's tax state as analytical instrument is a complement to standard economic theory, when this theory cannot apply. Schumpeter designed the concept to be used for the analysis of questions that require a long-term approach, because developments need to be analyzed that change the structures in which economic activity takes place. In modern terminology, Schumpeter's concept of the tax state is a concept needed in constitutional public finance. Whenever decisions have to be made about the structure of a country, a tax system, a particular sector, such as the health industry, or an international organization, such as the E.C., his analysis can be used. A tax state approach can shed light on consequences that are, in the long run, decisive for the performance of a country, an industry, or a particular institution, but that cannot be brought out by standard economic analysis. We can therefore expect tax state approaches to be particularly useful in exploratory types of work and in the case of trying to integrate interdisciplinary research efforts.

REFERENCES

Auerbach, Allen J., and Martin Feldstein. 1985. *Handbook of Public Economics*. Vol. 1. Amsterdam: North Holland.
Auerbach, Allen J., and Martin Feldstein. 1987. *Handbook of Public Economics*. Vol. 2. Amsterdam: North Holland.
Backhaus, Jürgen. 1980. "The Pareto Principle." *Analyse und Kritik* 2:146–71.
Backhaus, Jürgen. 1981. "The Pareto Principle." *Analyse und Kritik* 3:237–46.
Backhaus, Jürgen. 1989. "Taxation and Entrepreneurship: An Austrian Approach to Public Finance." *Journal of Economic Studies* 16(2):5–22.
Berding, Helmut, ed. 1981. *Privatkapital, Staatsfinanzen und Reformpolitik im Deutschland der napoleonischen Zeit*. Ostfildern: Scripta Mercaturae Verlag.
Eheberg, K. R. T. von. 1900. "Finanzen und Finanzwirtschaft." In *Handwörterbuch der Staatswissenschaften*, Vol. 3. Jena: Gustav Fischer, 902–36.

---

25. On November 19, 1919, Wieser wrote in his diary: "Kelsen tells me that the younger economists who considered him their leader have now given up on him as a scholar and do not expect anything from him anymore." Reprinted in Schumpeter 1992, 10.

Endres, M. 1900. "Forstpolitik." In *Handwörterbuch der Staatswissenschaften,* Vol. 3. Jena: Gustav Fischer, 1150–86.

Goldscheid, Rudolf. 1917. *Staatssozialismus oder Staatskapitalismus: Ein finanz-soziologischer Beitrag zur Lösung des Staatsschuldenproblems.* Vienna: Anzengruber.

Greve, Klaus, and Kersten Krüger. 1982. "Steuerstaat und Sozialstruktur— Finanzsoziologische Auswertung der hessischen Katastervorbeschreibungen für Waldkappel 1744 und Heerleshausen 1748." *Geschichte und Gesellschaft. Zeitschrift für Historische Sozialwissenschaft* 8(3):295–332.

Hennipman, Peter. 1980. "Some Notes on Pareto Optimality and Wicksellian Unanimity." In *Wandlungen in Wirtschaft und Gesellschaft,* ed. Emil Küng. Tübingen: Mohr (Siebeck).

Hennipman, Peter. 1982. "Wicksell and Pareto. Their Relationship in the Thought of Public Finance." *History of Political Economy* 14(1):37–64.

Hickel, Rudolf, ed. 1976. *Die Finanzkrise des Steuerstaates: Beiträge zur politischen Ökonomie der Staatsfinanzen.* Frankfurt: Suhrkamp.

Küng, Emil, ed. 1980. *Wandlungen in Wirtschaft und Gesellschaft: Die Wirt-schafts- und die Sozialwissenschaften vor neuen Aufgaben—Festschrift für Walter Adolf Jöhr.* Tübingen: Mohr (Siebeck).

Leibenstein, Harvey. 1962 "Notes on Welfare Economics and the Theory of Democracy." *Economic Journal* 72:299–319.

Mann, Fritz Karl. [1937] 1978. *Steuerpolitische Ideale.* Jena: Gustav Fischer. Reprint: Stuttgart, 1978, chapter 4.

Musgrave, Richard A. 1980. *Leviathan Commeth—or Does He?* Discussion Paper # 744, Cambridge, Mass.: Harvard Institute of Economic Research.

Musgrave, Richard A. 1985, 1987. "A Brief History of Fiscal Doctrine." In *Handbook of Public Economics,* ed. Auerbach and Feldstein, 1–54. Amsterdam: North Holland.

Musgrave, Richard A. 1992. "Schumpeter's Crisis of the Tax State: An Essay in Fiscal Sociology." *Journal of Evolutionary Economics* 2, no. 2 (August): 89–113.

Musgrave, Richard A., and Peggy B. Musgrave. 1989. *Public Finance in Theory and Practice.* 5th ed, New York: McGraw Hill.

Musgrave, Richard A., and Allan T. Peacock, eds. 1958. *Classics in the Theory of Public Finance.* London: Macmillan.

O'Connor, James. 1973. *The Fiscal Crisis of the State.* New York: St. Martin's Press.

Pareto, Vilfredo. 1935. *The Mind and Society.* New York: Harcourt Brace & Comp.

Rimpler. 1900. "Geschichte der Domänen." In *Handwörterbuch der Staats-wissenschaften,* Vol. 3. Jena: Gustav Fischer, 194–205.

Samuelson, Paul A. 1954. "The Pure Theory of Public Expenditure." *Review of Economics and Statistics* 36:387–89.

Schmoller, Gustav. 1863. "Die Lehre vom Einkommen in ihrem Zusammenhang mit den Grundprinzipien der Steuerlehre." *Zeitschrift für die gesammte Staatswissenschaft* 19:1–68.

Schmoller, Gustav. 1877. "Die Epochen der Preussischen Finanzpolitik." *Schmollers Jahrbuch,* N.F. 1.
Schumpeter, Joseph A. 1918a. "Die Krise des Steuerstaates." *Zeitfragen aus dem Gebiet der Soziologie.* Vol. 4. Graz and Leibzig: Leuschner and Lubensky. Reprinted in Schumpeter 1953, 1–71.
Schumpeter, Joseph A. 1918b. "Die Krise des Steuerstaates." *Zeitfragen aus dem Gebiet der Soziologie.* Vol. 4. Graz and Leibzig: Leuschner and Lubensky. Reprinted in Hickel 1976, 329–79.
Schumpeter, Joseph A. 1918c. "Die Krise des Steuerstaates." *Zeitfragen aus dem Gebiet der Soziologie.* Vol. 4. Graz and Leibzig: Leuschner and Lubensky. Reprinted in Swedburg 1991, 99–140.
Schumpeter, Joseph A. 1927. "Sombarts dritter Band." *Schmollers Jahrbuch für Gesetzgebung, Verwaltung und Volkswirtschaft im Deutschen Reiche* 51, 1, no. 3, 349–69.
Schumpeter, Joseph A. 1939. *Business Cycles: A Theoretical, Historical and Statistical Analysis of the Capitalist Process.* New York: McGraw-Hill.
Schumpeter, Joseph A. 1953. *Aufsätze zur Soziologie.* Tübingen: Mohr (Siebeck).
Schumpeter, Joseph A. 1954a. *History of Economic Analysis.* New York: Oxford University Press.
Schumpeter, Joseph A. 1954b. "Die Krise des Steuerstaates." Trans. by Wolfgang F. Stolper and Richard A. Musgrave. *International Economic Papers.* 4:5–38.
Schumpeter, Joseph A. 1970. *Das Wesen des Geldes.* Göttingen: Vandenhoeck & Ruprecht.
Schumpeter, Joseph A. 1985a. *Aufsätze zur Wirtschaftspolitik.* Tübingen: Mohr (Siebeck).
Schumpeter, Joseph A. 1985b. "Ökonomie und Soziologie der Einkommensteuer." In *Aufsätze zur Wirtschaftspolitik,* Joseph A. Schumpeter, 123–33. Tübingen: Mohr (Siebeck).
Schumpeter, Joseph A. 1985c. "Geist und Technik der Finanzverwaltung." In *Aufsätze zur Wirtschaftspolitik,* Joseph A. Schumpeter, 77–83. Tübingen: Mohr (Siebeck).
Schumpeter, Joseph A. 1992. *Politische Reden.* Ed. by Wolfgang F. Stolper and Christian Seidl. Tübingen: Mohr (Siebeck).
Smith, Adam. 1776. *The Wealth of Nations.* New York: Dutton.
Sombart, Werner. 1927. *Der Moderne Kapitalismus.* Vols. 1–3. Munich/Leipzig: Duncker & Humblot.
Sombart, Werner. 1933. "Capitalism." In *Encyclopedia of the Social Sciences.* Vol. 3. New York: Macmillan, 195–208.
Spiethoff, Arthur. 1933. "Die Allgemeine Volkswirtschaftslehre als geschichtliche Theorie: die Wirtschaftsstile." In *Festgabe für Werner Sombart zur Siebenzigsten Wiederkehr seines Geburtstages. Neunzehnter Jänner,* ed. Arthur Spiethoff, 51–84. München: Duncker & Humblot.
Stiglitz, Joseph. 1988. *Economics of the Public Sector.* 2d ed, New York: W. W. Norton.

Stopler, W. F., and R. A. Musgrave, eds. 1954. *International Economic Papers.* London: Macmillan.

Swedberg, Richard, ed. 1991. *Joseph A. Schumpeter: The Economics and Sociology of Capitalism.* Princeton, N. J.: Princeton University Press.

Tenzel, Christian. 1685. *Entdeckte Gold-Grube in der Accise.* Zerbst: Johann Lüderwaldt.

Umpfenbach. 1859, 1860. *Lehrbuch der Finanzwissenschaft.* 2 vols. Stuttgart: Erlangen. 1887.

[von Cölln, Georg Friedrich Willibald Ferdinand.] 1807. *Vertraute Briefe über die Inneren Verhältnisse am Preussischen Hofe seit dem Tode Friedrichs II.* Amsterdam/Cologne: Peter Hammer.

Wagner, Adolph. 1864. *Die Ordnung des österreichischen Staatshaushalts. 1863.* Vienna: Christian Brandstatter.

Wagner, Richard E. 1983. *Public Finance: Revenues and Expenditures in a Democratic Society.* Boston: Little Brown.

Wicksell, Knut. 1896. "Über ein neues Prinzip der gerechten Besteuerung." In *Finanztheoretische Untersuchungen.* Jena: Gustav Fischer. Partly translated (by James M. Buchanan) in Musgrave and Peacock 1958.

Witt, Peter Christian. 1970. *Die Finanzpolitik des Deutschen Reiches von 1903 bis 1913.* Lübeck: Matthiesen Verlag.

Witzleben, Alexander von. 1985. *Staatsfinanznot und sozialer Wandel. Eine finanzsoziologische Analyse der preußischen Reformzeit zu Beginn des 19. Jahrhunderts.* Stuttgart: Franz Steiner Verlag Wiesbaden GmbH.

Wolff, Christian (Freiherr von). 1754. *Grundsätze des Natur-und Völckerrechts.* Halle: Renger.

Schumpeter and Keynes: An Early Confrontation

Cornelius W. A. M. van Paridon

Without any doubt, both John Maynard Keynes and Joseph Alois Schumpeter have strongly influenced economic theory and economic policy in the twentieth century. They published important books and articles, often on similar issues, like monetary theory, economic policies, and business cycles. While Keynes directed his attention mostly to short-term developments, Schumpeter was attracted by the long-term development of capitalist economies. With hindsight, it seems that each of their approaches could have benefited from the insights and ideas of the other. Living in about the same era (1883–1946 or 1950, respectively), there could have been ample opportunities to meet one another and to cooperate together. However fruitful such a cooperation between these two giants could have been, in reality the contacts were scarce and rather cool.

The relationship between Keynes and Schumpeter is the central theme of this contribution. It is discussed on the basis of an article Schumpeter published in 1925 in a Dutch weekly, *Economisch-Statistische Berichten*.[1] It was written in Dutch.[2] The article was based on a lecture Schumpeter had given in Rotterdam in 1925. In this lecture, Schumpeter criticized the Keynes's ideas for a managed currency, and favored instead the Gold Standard.[3]

After presenting information regarding this lecture, its main content is described. Thereafter, its influence on Dutch monetary thinking and its impact on economic theory regarding the relationship between monetary variables and economic development is treated. Finally, the strenuous relationship between Schumpeter and Keynes will be discussed.

---

1. The article has been translated by this author into English, with the title *Old and New Banking Policy*. It is included in this volume.

2. The author learned very recently that this article has also been translated into German by H.-J. Wagener. It was published in Seidl and Stolper 1992.

3. In that same period, Schumpeter published several articles on the same issue. See Schumpeter 1925b, 1927, and 1928.

Schumpeter in the Netherlands

Early in 1925, Schumpeter came to Bonn to accept an offer from the University of Bonn to become Professor of Public Finance. In the years after the Great War he had been Minister of Finance for less than eight months and head of a private bank, which eventually collapsed in 1927. Neither job had brought him the success Schumpeter himself, and certainly many others, had expected from this exceptionally bright man. He held this chair for 7 years. He left Bonn in 1932, going to Harvard.

The Netherlands School of Economics, founded in 1913, then had a very active student community.[4] Earlier, W. Rathenau had been invited by the same students' union for a lecture. Now the students used the proximity of Bonn (about 200 miles) to invite the then already-famous Schumpeter for a lecture. Maybe the willingness of Schumpeter to accept the invitation was related to the fact that just before, G. M. Verrijn Stuart, the son of professor C. A. Verrijn Stuart, the best-known Dutch economist in Austria at that time, had been appointed to Rotterdam. Another argument for the invitation could have been that after the reintroduction of the Gold Standard, in April, 1925, the public discussion on this issue had nearly completely disappeared.[5] The ideas of Keynes were judged to have no practical relevance. For people like both of the Verrijn Stuarts, this invitation to Schumpeter meant a nice opportunity to restart that discussion.

Instrumental to this invitation was S. Posthuma, who had just received his M.A. from this School. He had just been appointed as editor of the *Economisch-Statistische Berichten,* a Dutch weekly published by the Netherlands Economic Institute, the research department of the Netherlands School of Economics. Schumpeter stayed at the house of the parents of Posthuma. The text of the lecture was subsequently published in *Economisch-Statistische Berichten,* in Dutch.[6]

---

4. Some of the information mentioned here is based on private communication of the author with Prof. H. W. Lambers, a student and later a professor at the Netherlands School of Economics. He was also editor of the *Economisch-Statistische Berichten,* the periodical that published Schumpeter's lecture. See also Lambers 1981.

5. This information is from Prof. Lambers. Its dating of the lecture differs from that of Wagener. Wagener states that Schumpeter gave his lecture before April 28, 1925, the date of the return to the Gold Standard (Wagener 1992, 12). Schumpeter's text gives no clue as to which interpretation is the correct one.

6. It is not known whether Schumpeter provided a translated text, or whether it was translated by Posthuma or someone else.

Old and New Banking Policy

The article is a plea by Schumpeter for a return to the gold standard. He states that the arguments on the general benefits of the gold standard, the consideration for the vested interests (and in particular for the issuing banks), and the arguments on the relative simplicity, the comprehensibility and the ease of reorganizing finance inherent in a return to gold, speak for themselves. But the return to gold is not merely an effective measure in monetary terms. Gold and its movement provides, in the very extent to which this is automatic or can again become so (and on the very road toward this), the most effective mechanism available at present for solving a number of nonmonetary economic, political, and social problems. The free gold standard could help Europe to overcome its crisis, could help America to get used to its new position, could bring peoples closer together, could enforce peaceful cooperation on pain of immediately felt economic losses, could aid groups of disadvantaged workers in their fight for better living conditions, and much more (Schumpeter 1992, 24).

When discussing the ideas of Keynes, Schumpeter (1992, 6) states that Keynes has a different objective, namely, the stability of the price level. The banking methods available are the same with the new policy as with the old one: bank-rate policy, open-market operations, influencing the percentage of cover, exercising discrimination when granting credit. It is true that these instruments were now to take on a different character: under the old system they were temporary aids for rectifying faults in a fundamentally automatic competitive mechanism, which should basically, and in the absence of national and international political and economic-political tensions (which always provoke quasi-mercantilist measures) require no intervention according to any kind of fixed scheme. In the new system, the reverse should be the case, with this intervention forming the foundation. Automatism would be abolished, in principle, and capitalist society would, in this way, acquire a central institution that would make the necessary decisions, both consciously and according to a fixed scheme. Its nerve cords would be those very same instruments of banking policy whose effects Keynes would like to see reinforced by modifying the circulation of bank notes, again according to a fixed scheme. This is tantamount to saying that the central bank would become absolute master over the general economic situation. The bank would be able to set the price level at any desirable rate or, for example, hold it constant. Schumpeter concludes that a Central Bank would technically be able to fulfill such a policy.

This does not mean, however, that Schumpeter, therefore, accepts the full consequences of the argument. On the contrary, there are three main points which lead Schumpeter to the rejection of the Keynesian ideas.

The first point is Schumpeter's observation that acceptance of the proposals of Keynes would mean, in principle, the unlimited regulation of the whole economic life of a society, and, therefore, an actual limitation of the possibilities of private initiative and a marked deviation from the economic principles of private property and free competition. The decision on what is to be produced, and how, would, from now on, be in the hands of a central body; the same would apply to the distribution of the proceeds of production among the various social classes. Considering that the international movement of capital, which is now an important regulator of the economic-political objectives of all governments, would also fall under the control of this central body, it would mean an end to the automatic functioning and automatic development of the world economy (Schumpeter 1992, 8).

The second point, then, is the observation that automatism has to be chosen above discretionary policy. Automatism means that protectionist tendencies have less chances to appear (Schumpeter 1992, 23). It prevents, furthermore, the trend toward further intervention, as indicated above. Why should banking policy only be directed at the stabilization of the price level? In countries where agriculture exerts considerable political power, it has managed to procure credit advantages to which it has no right, according to purely business principles. In more general terms, there exists a tendency to use credit facilities to increase employment or to bring down unemployment. Schumpeter (1992, 6) draws attention to the fact that there are many other issues besides unemployment that can be regulated in such a way. For instance, one could subordinate this banking policy to the notion of the preservation of a country's natural resources. Finally, there is no single national, sociopolitical aim—intensification of agriculture, arms production or suppression, the stimulation of house construction, antinarcotics activities—that could not be included in the sphere of the new banking policy. Also, discretionary policies are always too late and never adjusted to the particular circumstances.

The third point is that the main economic policy goal, as proposed by Keynes, the stabilization of the price level, is not desirable, according to Schumpeter, because it interferes negatively with the necessary business cycle developments. Keynes claimed that the changes in the money volume are the causes of evil (Schumpeter 1992, 13). That is to say: the credit policy of the banks is the sole cause of prosperity and depression. Expansion of credit encourages both good and bad firms alike, conjures up visions of profits through the price movements it instigates, even if they do not already exist, and leads to an irrational expansion of production and speculative excesses. Contraction of credit, which moreover occurs merely as a consequence of the necessity to exchange bank deposits for legal currency, therefore makes an end to all of this, both far too late and far too drastically, puts pressure on the price level, brings both good and bad enterprises to a standstill, and induces unemployment. This is, therefore, a completely pointless state of affairs, an unadulterated ill, that must clearly be combatted by means of a banking policy as soon as the opportunity to do so presents itself.

Schumpeter considers this claim to be incorrect. Not because he doubts that economic fluctuations can be averted through credit policy. Nor because he queries the proposition that the rise in price level during a period of prosperity and its fall during a depression is directly caused by monetary events. But simply because Schumpeter is of the opinion that both prosperity and depression fulfill an essential role and that, in turn, expansion and contraction of credit are important "actors," very difficult to replace. In other words: it is not Keynes's monetary theory that Schumpeter contests, but his theory on the trade cycle.

By a credit-expanding and credit-contracting neutralizing modification of the circulation of bank notes—the discount policy alone would not be sufficient here—fluctuations in the price level could be averted. This would not only result in the simple elimination of a fault in the credit machine; a part of this machine, so essential to the national economy, would be paralyzed. Because it is these temporary deviations from the parallelism between the flow of goods and the means of circulation, this periodic inflation and deflation of credit, that constitute the very method by which the economic organization of economic progress, resting on private property, competition, and credit, is conducted, its results become absorbed into the normal cycle. The inflation of credit during a period of prosperity diverts, through the rise in price level that it causes, part of the available means of production from the targets to which they had been consigned so far, and makes them available for new men and new goals. If one wished to dismiss this process, then one would have to be consistent in preventing the import of foreign capital, which has, broadly speaking, the same purpose. Both the relative and the absolute deflation of credit during a slump restore not only the normal relation between commodities and circulation. The fall in prices leads, on the one hand, to a rise in the real income of consumers, thereby allowing the whole population to taste the fruits of the boom; on the other hand, it casts aside the superseded, thereby realizing the achievements of the boom for the structure of production of the national economy (Schumpeter 1992, 18).

This whole process does not occur without shocks. Neither does it take place in the ideal manner. The uncertainty regarding the ultimate success of the new and its effects on the old (and therefore on all economic factors) that reigns during the course of this process of absorption, which in turn constitutes the essence of the slump, means that while much of the old and antiquated survives, given adequate support, much of what is healthy and vigorous perishes. The precautionary measures taken on all sides lead to temporary restrictions of production and, thereby, to a higher increase in unemployment than necessary. An argument in favor of a more discriminating crisis therapy would therefore not be completely unjustified. But an attack on the fundaments of the whole process would, given this state of affairs, serve to check economic progress unless accompanied by many more reforms in the capitalist economy (Schumpeter 1992, 19).

Even though Schumpeter admitted that the gold standard was not an ideal, in itself, he was unable to accept the observation that people were seeking to reject it right at the moment when it was about to do mankind a great—and perhaps final—service.

Schumpeter and Dutch Monetarist Thinking[7]

Schumpeter's article certainly has left its traces in Dutch monetary thinking. Fase even speaks of "the rise of Dutch monetarism" in this respect (Fase 1991). The debate started immediately after Schumpeter's lecture, through a response from J. G. Koopmans. He wanted this reaction to be published in *Economisch-Statistische Berichten*. Its editor, S. Posthuma, was worried by this request, not only because of the status of Schumpeter, but also because he opposed Koopmans's views. He was able to redirect this article to *De Economist* (Koopmans 1925). Posthuma (1926) published a reply in the same journal.[8]

Koopmans emphasized that the main differences between Schumpeter and Keynes were with their business cycle analysis and policy recommendations. Whereas Schumpeter considered price fluctuations as a necessary signal of adjustments to changing circumstances, Keynes viewed it as a danger, when the prices should go down. Koopmans had similar fears: new ideas, new entrepreneurs would imply a higher demand for credits. When this demand should be met through artificial instead of natural sources, then the economy would go into disequilibrium. To prevent such an unwanted situation, a strict monetary policy

---

7. This section is strongly based on Fase 1991. See also Wagener 1992.
8. See Lambers 1981, 109.

should be applied to realize a stable price level. In a later article, Koopmans (1933) connected this view with that of *neutrales geld,* neutral money. The basic principle of neutrality was that monetary authorities should try to use monetary policy in such a way that the real, money-using economy should equal as much as possible that of an ideal barter economy. Money should not exert any independent influence.

This approach created a lively debate in the Netherlands in the thirties, with J. Tinbergen, C. A. Verrijn Stuart, and G. M. Verrijn Stuart as important contributors. It did not result, then, in an operational criterion for monetary policy. Twenty years later, however, M. W. Holtrop, president of the Nederlandsche Bank (the Dutch Central Bank) introduced a new diagnostic method to analyze monetary fluctuations. He based this approach on the ideas of Koopmans. According to Koopmans, a necessary and sufficient condition for the occurrence of any monetary equilibrium is that the algebraic sum of spontaneous inflationary and deflationary disturbances should be zero (Fase 1991, 12). Holtrop tried to translate this concept into a workable framework. Again, this approach created a debate, this time between Tinbergen, Witteveen, Koopmans, and Holtrop. The method was applied by Holtrop. It enabled the Bank to recognize the origin and character of monetary disturbances in the Dutch economy and to approximately delineate the responsibilities (Fase 1991, 13). When Holtrop retired in 1969, he decided to analyze his own experiences with this approach through an econometric evaluation (Holtrop 1972). This evaluation was strongly criticized by Selden (1975). From his American monetarist perspective, he had serious doubts, not only about Holtrop's empirical testing, but also because Holtrop's approach was contrary to the quantity theory tradition, even though Holtrop started from the same theoretical base (Fase 1991, 14).

Schumpeter and the Importance of Monetary Issues

One of the main lessons of Schumpeter's paper on old and new banking policy is that monetary policy is an essential ingredient to stimulate entrepreneurial behavior, in the widest sense, and so to bring about economic development. It seems that this lesson has been too much neglected.

Whatever has been left of the Keynesian revolution, monetary policy along monetarist lines, however moderate, has been a generally accepted approach. Such a monetary policy has been judged as an essential prerequisite for a sound economic development, especially as the effort toward price stability has been combined with an independent

Central Bank. An attractive example of such a combination is the German Bundesbank. Its performance regarding price stability has been so good that the European Central Bank, foreseen in the treaty of Maastricht on Economic and Monetary Union, is predicted to become a European equivalent of the Bundesbank. This combination of a monetary policy aimed in the first place at price stability and in an institutional framework that guarantees its independence, seems an attractive compromise between Keynes and Schumpeter. Whereas Keynes stressed the necessity for price stability, to be realized through adequate monetary policy, Schumpeter feared that such a policy would mean the first step on the road toward socialism. Through creating an independent institution, however, solely aimed at price stability, this road can effectively be blocked. Still, this compromise is not able to correct the main criticism of Schumpeter, namely, that price stability is at odds with change, and with economic development.

Recently, several authors have emphasized this peculiar relationship, basing their argument on the Schumpeterian line of thinking. Tichy (1984) states that the monetary theory of Schumpeter is an unjustly neglected part of his work. This certainly is connected with the fact that Schumpeter did not publish, during his lifetime, a book on this issue, even though he had been very active on this issue in the period between 1925 and 1932, during his stay in Bonn.[9] Tichy (1984, 137) gives several arguments about why this publication did not appear, namely, that Schumpeter had difficulties with the formulation of a chapter on a genuine dynamic monetary theory, that he believed that his earlier work in this field was refused by the profession, as well as by the general public, and that Keynes disturbed Schumpeter's work by publishing, in 1930, his *Treatise on Money*. This last aspect will be dealt with later on.

Naderer (1990) gives an extensive description of Schumpeter's view of the monetary aspects of the process of economic development. She concludes that Schumpeter's contribution has not lost its value for explaining current economic developments and for suggesting relevant policy proposals. Zinn (1983) supports the vision of Schumpeter that an anti-inflationary monetary policy slows down economic development. A sufficient monetary supply that is not tied to strict counterinflation policy is a necessary precondition for upswings that form the links in the chain of economic development. Streissler (1984), too, stresses, with a Schumpeterian view, the role of banks and their credit policies in stimulating innovations and, so, economic development. Bellofiore (1985) de-

---

9. The book was finally published in 1970, in an edited version. See Schumpeter 1970.

scribes the consequences of Schumpeter's monetary ideas for the understanding of the accumulation process, as well as its relationship with the Marxian approach toward this subject. Schumpeter sees capitalism as a structurally unstable process, due to the endogeneity of innovations and, as a consequence, of money supply. Bellofiore views Schumpeter's contributions as a more appropriate critical reference for a renewal of Marxian theory of value than Ricardian or neo-Ricardian theories. Where Schumpeter once described his approach as a proper alternative for Keynesian ideas that would ultimately end in socialism, he certainly should not have expected that his own alternative would be judged appropriate for a Marxian renewal.

One final remark about monetary policy and its consequences for long-term economic development. As has been said, there currently exists a more or less general consensus that a sound monetary development, a growth of the monetary supply that does not lead to inflation, is a prerequisite for prosperous economic development. Even though this statement has not been disputed, it should be noted that each choice has its price. It has been argued, in the debate about the European Monetary Union, that such a policy could be detrimental to employment opportunities, especially in the short run. That cost was accepted. It seems to me that the article by Schumpeter put forward another cost that has been neglected so far, namely, the increased difficulty in realizing innovations and bringing about sufficient structural changes. This raises the question of whether banks and other financial intermediaries are able to finance high-risk experiments in different countries, whether they are allowed to do so by their Central Banks and their monetary authorities, and what impact this has on economic growth, and, more precisely, on economic development. Whatever positive remarks can be made about German monetary policy and its low inflation rate, at the same time, this country has been criticized in the last decade for its rigidities. Some observers even fear that Germany is increasingly lagging behind in technological developments. Of course, this is no evidence for the correctness of Schumpeter's views, but it is certainly one of the elements that should be taken into account.

Schumpeter and Keynes

It is remarkable how pronounced the differences between Schumpeter and Keynes appear to be, revealing themselves from this discussion. More than a decade after the publication of "The General Theory of Employment, Interest and Money," it seems that the two authors had already taken their position. The General Theory got much more attention than Schumpeter's "Business Cycles." Both publications dealt with the economic crisis of the thirties. Whereas Keynes had a short-term, demand-oriented approach, Schumpeter tried to explain the period and the severity of the crisis out of the occurrence of a long-wave-like development pattern. Not only was Keynes three years ahead, but also, because of its more practical relevance, both economists and policymakers preferred his book to that of Schumpeter.

This outcome was rather disappointing for Schumpeter. According to several authors, such as Haberler (1950) and Giersch (1984), the perceived lack of attention and of appreciation of his own contribution hit his idle character rather strongly. Schumpeter himself had been highly critical of the General Theory. In his review, Schumpeter (1936) mentioned four crucial points in this respect, namely the time- and place-restrictedness, the lighthearted use of economic aggregates, the assumption of a given technology, and the negative judgment of Keynes on an unequal income distribution (Giersch 1984, 104). Most profoundly, his criticism was directed at the heart of the Keynesian approach, namely that a reasonable government was able to pursue an economic policy, as restricted as necessary and as extensive as usable, to realize its main goals. Schumpeter had the opinion that a first step in this direction would ultimately lead to socialism. This judgment Schumpeter had already given, one decade earlier, in the paper that is the focus of this article.

Schumpeter and Keynes were both very prominent economists, highly esteemed inside and outside the economics discipline. They had a certain admiration for one another, yet their scientific and personal relationship was rather difficult and strenuous. The little story in Perlman's comments is illustrative enough (Perlman 1994, 127). This can partly be traced back to major scientific differences. Krelle (1984) was able to list twelve of these differences. Keynes was more the economist, with attention mainly to the short run; to demand, consumption, and employment; more pessimistic about the long run; pro government intervention; and had no interest in history or long-term business cycles— that is, he held a static view of economic development. Schumpeter was more the social scientist, attracted by the long run and optimistic about it, with a dynamic view and with much interest in structural changes, investment, and history—that is, for economic development, instead of economic growth. Of course, these differences are profound and important, yet they still do not make it clear why Schumpeter was so sharp, so abrasive even (Perlman 1994, 127) about Keynes.

Of course, for someone born after Keynes and Schumpeter died, it is difficult to provide an acceptable explanation for this behavior of

Schumpeter. Maybe Schumpeter envied Keynes's institutional security, his savoir faire, his position in the public debate, and his success with the General Theory, as Perlman (1994, 127) states. But it seems that there is more. According to Elliott (1985, 7), Schumpeter was disappointed by the ignorance of English-speaking economists of his *Theorie der wirtschaftlichen Entwicklung*. Published just before WWI in the German language, it was only after the English translation in 1934 that it got full attention. Furthermore, Schumpeter's assessment of the easier, or more rapid achievement, of practical success by such economists as Marshall and Keynes combined admiration with reproof and, on occasion, a trace of condescension, as Elliott (1985, 23) describes.

This antagonistic behavior toward Keynes certainly contributed to the relative neglect of Schumpeter's approach during his lifetime and long thereafter in economics and in the economic policy arena. Only recently have his ideas been picked up again by these people. It certainly has been a pity that this revival has taken so long, not only because theorizing along Schumpeterian lines has been nearly absent for such a long time, but also because Schumpeter's behavior made it impossible to work at an integration of his views with those of Keynes. As already stated, the approaches complemented one another quite well. If such an integration had been realized in the fifties, it could have led to an economic policy appropriate both for the short and the long run. Not only did Schumpeter prevent closer contact with Keynes because of this behavior, he also negatively influenced the integration of his views with the dominant paradigm. Of course, as Keynes himself asked, in the introduction of The General Theory, "forgiveness if, in the pursuit of sharp distinctions, my controversy is itself too keen" (Keynes 1936, V). Schumpeter was, at certain occasions, not only too keen, but also did not seem to be bothered by it. If so, then this has had regrettable consequences for the impact of his approach on economic theory.

BIBLIOGRAPHY

Bellofiore, Riccardo. 1985. "Money and Development in Schumpeter." *Review of Radical Political Economics* 17:21–40.
Bös, Dieter, und Hans-Dieter Stolper. 1984. *Schumpeter oder Keynes? Zur Wirtschaftspolitik der neunziger Jahre*. Berlin: Springer Verlag.
Elliott, John E. 1985. "Schumpeter's Theory of Economic Development and Social Change: Exposition and Assessment." *International Journal of Social Economy* 12:6–33.

Fase, Martin M. G. 1991. *Schumpeter and the Rise of Dutch Monetarism.* Paper prepared for the meeting of the History of Economics Society, 15–17 June 1991, at the University of Maryland.

Frisch, Helmut, ed. 1984. *Schumpeterian Economics.* New York: Praeger.

Giersch, Herbert. 1984. "The Age of Schumpeter." *American Economic Review Papers and Proceedings* 74:103–9.

Haberler, Gottfried. 1950. "Joseph Alois Schumpeter." *Quarterly Journal of Economics* 64:333–72.

Holtrop, M. W. 1972. "On the Effectiveness of Monetary Policy: The Experience of the Netherlands in the Years 1954–1969." *Journal of Money, Credit and Banking* 4:283–311.

Keynes, J. M. 1930. *Treatise on Money.* London: Macmillan.

Keynes, John M. 1936. *The General Theory of Employment, Interest of Money.* London: Macmillan.

Koopmans, J. G. 1925. "De zin der bankpolitiek: Schumpeter contra Keynes" (The Meaning of Banking Policy: Schumpeter vs Keynes). *De Economist* 74:798–818.

Koopmans, J. G. 1933. "Zum Problem des neutralen Geldes." In *Beiträge zur Geldtheorie,* ed. F. A. Hayek. Wien: Julius Springer.

Krelle, Wilhelm. 1984. "Keynes und Schumpeter: Unterschiedliche Ansätze." In *Schumpeter oder Keynes? Zur Wirtschaftspolitik der neunziger Jahre,* ed. Dieter Bös und Hans-Dieter Stolper. Berlin: Springer Verlag.

Lambers, Hendrik W. 1981. "The Vision." In *Schumpeter's Vision; Capitalism, Socialism and Democracy after 40 years,* ed. Arnold Heertje. New York: Praeger Publishers.

Naderer, Bärbel. 1990. *Die Entwicklung der Geldtheorie Joseph A. Schumpeters; Statische und dynamische Theorie des Geldes im kapitalistischen Marktsystem.* Berlin: Duncker & Humblot.

Perlman, Mark. 1994. "Commentary" on "Schumpeter and Keynes: An Early Confrontation" by C. W. A. M. van Paridon. In this volume.

Posthuma, S. 1926. "De zin der bankpolitiek" (The Meaning of Banking Policy). *De Economist* 75:423–58.

Schumpeter, Joseph A. 1925a. "Nieuwe en oude bankpolitiek" (New and Old Banking Policy). *Economisch-Statistische Berichten.* 10:552–54, 574–77, and 600–601. See also Schumpeter (1992).

Schumpeter, Joseph A. 1925b. "Kreditkontrolle." *Archiv für Sozialwissenschaften und Sozialpolitik* 54:289–328.

Schumpeter, Joseph A. 1927. "Die goldene Bremse an der Kreditmaschine." *Die Kreditwirtschaft* 1:80–106.

Schumpeter, Joseph A. 1928. "The Instability of Capitalism." *Economic Journal* 38:361–86.

Schumpeter, Joseph A. 1936. "Book Review of The General Theory of Employment, Interest and Money." *Journal of the American Statistical Association* 31:791–95.

Schumpeter, Joseph A. 1939. *Business Cycles.* London: Macmillan.

Schumpeter, Joseph A. 1970. *Das Wesen des Geldes.* Göttingen: Vandenhoeck & Ruprecht.

Schumpeter, Joseph A. 1992. "Old and New Banking Policy." In *Innovation in Technology, Industries, and Institutions: Comparative Perspectives,* ed. Mark Perlman. Ann Arbor, Mich.:University of Michigan Press.

Seidl, Christian, ed. 1984. *Lectures on Schumpeterian Economics; Schumpeterian Centenary Memorial Lectures, Graz 1983.* Berlin: Springer Verlag.

Seidl, Christian, und Wolfgang F. Stolper, eds. 1992. *Joseph A. Schumpeter; Tagespolitische Stellungnahmen.* Tübingen: J. C. B. Mohr (Paul Seibeck).

Selden, R. T. 1975. "A Critique of Dutch Monetarism." *Journal of Monetary Economics* 1:221–32.

Streissler, Erich. 1984. "Schumpeter's Vienna and the Role of Credit in Innovation." In *Schumpeterian Economics,* ed. Helmut Frisch. New York: Praeger.

Tichy, Günther. 1984. "Schumpeter's Monetary Theory: An Unjustly Neglected Part of his Work." In *Lectures on Schumpeterian Economics; Schumpeterian Centenary Memorial Lectures, Graz 1983,* ed. Chrisian Seidl. Berlin: Springer Verlag.

Wagener, Hans J. 1992. "Schumpeters Keynes-Attacke und die niederländischen Monetaristen." In *Joseph A. Schumpeter; Tagespolitische Stellungnahmen,* ed. Christian Seidl und Wolfgang F. Stolper. Tübingen: J. C. B. Mohr (Paul Siebeck).

Zinn, Karl G. 1983. "Zyklus, Stabilität und Geldneutralität; Eine lehrgeschichtliche Ergänzung zum Problem der potentialorientierten Geldpolitik auf der Grundlage von Schumpeters Entwicklungstheorie." *Konjunkturpolitik* 29: 329–47.

Old and New Banking Policy

Joseph A. Schumpeter

1

It was both obvious and inevitable that the consumption and destruction of commodities during the war and in the postwar period would be reflected in the monetary and credit systems of all countries, that the parallelism between money and goods flows would be disrupted, and that a situation would arise in which the normal principles of monetary and banking policy could not, at least temporarily, be applied. These principles are designed for normal conditions, in just the same way as all other basic principles of an economic organization based on private property and private initiative. No monetary policy could have altered the above-mentioned phenomena. And even if they could have been avoided, the question would still remain as to whether this would have been recorded as an unadulterated benefit. After all, the monetary events during the war were merely expressions of adaptations to the circumstances of the time. And if one has a sense of regret regarding the suffering that they brought, then one must not forget that these same phenomena which took the form of inflation in gold, credit, and paper currency, would otherwise have made themselves felt in other, and not necessarily less painful, ways. The sudden panic demand for war materials, for example, and the necessary, and welcome, reorientation of trade and industry toward new products and methods, or the sudden disappearance of large markets, would have been enough to lead to inflation (we wish to use this often misused term here in the sense of every deviation from the strict parallelism between money and goods flows), even if a state bill had never been issued; but even accepting that this could have been averted in one way or another, the

This article, written in Dutch, has been published in the Dutch weekly *Economisch-Statistische Berichten* 10 (1925) in three consecutive issues, namely, 1, no. 496: 552–54; 2, no. 497: 574–77; and 3, no. 498: 600–601. The article has been translated by C. W. A. M. van Paridon.

world would have nevertheless now been poorer and its economic organization shaken.

Despite this, it is very understandable how at present, as at the end of the Napoleonic wars, not only the question of how one can best return to normal conditions arises, but also the more far-reaching question as to whether or not a return should be made to prewar practice. The essentially new and fundamentally interesting aspect of the reform plan, which is associated with the name Keynes, does not lie in the fact that it recommends a freeing of money from gold and from a monetary policy based on the gold standard: we have long been aware that it is not theoretically essential that money consist of gold or be convertible to gold, and that gold falls far short of fulfilling its role in an ideal manner. It is even true to say that no system of gold coinage has ever functioned simply and automatically, but has always tended to be a "managed currency." Keynes and his supporters, however, tend to sail too lightly over the fact that the sense in which this is correct deviates significantly from that in which a monetary system without gold would have to be referred to in the same way. Were we, nevertheless, to reach the conclusion that a full and speedy return to the gold standard was advisable, given the present situation in the world, then this would rest exclusively on practical considerations, in particular on a relative "underestimation" of the disadvantages and dangers of such a return, as mentioned by Keynes, and not on theoretical differences of any kind. The new element in the reform plan does not lie in the limited emphasis that Keynes places on stabilization of the exchange rate. Nor is stabilization of the price level the point on which everything hinges. Nevertheless, this stabilization is the immediate objective of the reforms and features at the top of the reform agenda, as a consequence of which we will be paying it due attention below. However, the basic idea behind the reforms does go much further and deeper, and is independent of every specific aim as such: the idea, namely, of extending banking policy into a general therapy for the national economy, into an instrument by means of which the national economy can be regulated in a conscious way and according to a fixed scheme. The notion of replacing the automatism of economic organization based on free competition by conscious intervention according to a fixed scheme is already centuries old, of course. It has been presented to us in every conceivable theoretical and practical form: theoretically in its most radical form, of course, from the socialist camp, and practically most clearly by the new organizational creations of the war period. Yet Keynes's proposal is of a completely different standard, even in terms of intellectual motivation. And furthermore, it is original with respect to both the main issue and the method employed. In terms of this basic principle, the specific, practical objective that one wishes to achieve at any given moment by means of this technique becomes purely incidental: instead of stabilization of the price level, it could just as easily be the fight against alcoholism. In the presence of such an audacious thought, I will not be so uncharitable as to point out the obvious practical problems, especially where the plan distinguishes itself favorably from other such plans ith respect to practical application and a certain consideration for the important mainsprings of capitalist society.

However, I would like to formulate it as clearly as possible and with all its consequences. So far, the policy of a central bank has, by virtue of its nature, regulated its country's monetary and credit systems exclusively from the perspective of these special areas, and accordingly attempted to keep the value of the unit of purchasing power between the limits determined by the gold points and to influence the credit structure in such a way that this could have no influence on the gold parity. These perspectives would, according to the new policy, as supported by Keynes, cease to be the aim or even to have a significant meaning. The monetary and credit systems would become the slaves of general economic-political objectives. Old banking policy also took heed of the general symptoms of the economic situation, such as price level, unemployment, export figures, and so on, and it is not completely fair of Keynes to reproach it for having only been directed toward circulation, the gold flow, and such. However, it did, as a rule, only take account of the general economic situation and try to influence this in order to keep the monetary and credit systems safe and out of danger, the level of health being measured against the gold parity. In the new policy, circulation, percentage of cover, exchange rates, and so on, are not immaterial, either, although it does not aim at a particular magnitude or condition of these factors; it sees them as a means of influencing the economic situation and its development. Taking account of the gold flow would become inappropriate, given the idea of demonetizing gold inherent to this policy: the desire (with the completely free application of the tools of monetary and credit policy for steering one's national economy) not to be restricted by this consideration and, accordingly, to isolate national finances, as it were, in order to subject them fully to the economic will of domestic institutions, is, after all, the real basis for the proposal to demonetize.

The banking methods available are the same with the new policy as with the old one: bank-rate policy, open-market operations, influencing the percentage of cover, exercising discrimination when granting credit. It is true that these instruments are now to take on a different character: under the old system they were temporary aids for rectifying faults in a

fundamentally automatic competitive mechanism, which should basically, and in the absence of national and international political and
economic-political tensions (which always provoke quasi-mercantilist
measures) require no intervention according to any kind of fixed scheme.
In the new system the reverse should be the case, with this intervention
forming the foundation. Automatism would be abolished, in principle,
and capitalist society would, in this way, acquire a central institution that
would make the necessary decisions, both consciously and according to a
fixed scheme. Its nerve cords would be those very same instruments of
banking policy whose effects Keynes would like to see reinforced by
modifying the circulation of bank notes, again according to a fixed
scheme.

This is tantamount to saying that the central bank would become
absolute master over the general economic situation. It would be able to
set the price level at any desirable rate or, for example, hold it constant.
It is true that this does not apply to bank-rate policy, and when many
writers, as followers or supporters of Keynes, lay exclusive emphasis on
bank-rate policy, they add a great deal of water to the reform program
wine, although Keynes himself does not do so: if banking policy were to
take the form that he supports, then it would even be possible to convert
every economic upswing into a slump and every slump (by an inflationary injection, as it were) into an economic upswing, if one so desired.
The central bank would be able to prevent unemployment, or at least
reduce it to a reasonably constant minimum. It would become possible
to put a stop to panic and crises, on the one hand, and speculative
excesses, on the other. The relation between creditors and debtors
would be left to the judgment of the central bank. It would be left to the
bank's judgment to decide if the creditor was to receive a constant
quantity of consumers' goods or a constant share in the social product, a
premium above one or both of these standards or lower than the sum
demanded. Expansions and contractions in credit could be eased, neutralized, or overcompensated. Free from all obligations to take into
account the commitment to convert gold to cash, the central bank would
be able, at its own discretion, to carry out a resolute policy of inflation or
deflation—why the reformers can decry the improper printing of money
during wartime without actually being able to reject the method of
printing money itself—and set price level and exchange rates to suit
their desires. The objective that Keynes emphasizes is stability of the
price level. But in the same way that one can support the freeing of the
exchange rates and their flexible adaptation to the relevant economic
situation, one can use the same arguments to fight for elasticity of the

price level and to consider now a fall and then a rise of that level, given the economic-political and social situation of a nation, appropriate.

But that is not all. It is not only the general economic situation, but also every separate industry, viewed from whichever perspective one likes, that can be influenced by the new policy. This has happened from time to time in the past, but as exceptions to the rule, as it were. In countries where agriculture exerts considerable political power, it has managed to procure credit advantages to which it had no right according to purely business principles. In temporary states of emergency, many a central bank has helped many an industry in a way that strongly diverges from the normal rules relating to the assessment of the means of exchange, securities, and the banking situation. This must now become a fundamental principle. The recently published memorandum of the London "Industrial Institute" already provides a very nice example of the application of such economic "camphor injections" albeit very cautiously. It deals with the extension of credit facilities to enterprises in a position to employ more staff. We will not go into the question as to why industries rationally capable of expanding their operations should not also obtain the necessary credit without such facilities. We will merely draw attention to the fact that there are many other issues besides unemployment that can be regulated in such a way. One naturally thinks, for example, of Alfred Marshall's doctrine, that it is a good thing, under certain circumstances, to favor industries in which the law of increasing returns applies, at the expense of industries with diminishing returns. Or one could subordinate this banking policy to the notion of the preservation of a country's natural resources. And finally, there is no single national, sociopolitical, public health aim—intensification of agriculture, arms production or suppression, the stimulation of house construction, antinarcotics activities—that could not be included in the sphere of the new banking policy.

This is no longer management of the monetary system, but management of the whole national economy, without any visible boundaries. It means an actual limitation of the possibilities of private initiative and a marked deviation from the economic principles of private property and free competition. The decision on what is to be produced, and how, would, from now on, be in the hands of a central body: the same would apply to the distribution of the proceeds of production among the various social classes. And considering that the international movement of capital, which is now an important regulator of the economic-political objectives of all governments, would also fall under the control of this central body, it would mean an end to the automatic functioning and automatic development of the world economy. Many people will perhaps wonder if the time has not yet come to take this path. On the other hand, many will perhaps be of the opinion that, if the time really has come for such a political strategy, it would be more logical and more effective to immediately declare oneself the adherent of some practicable form of socialism. But this is of little significance to us. We are only concerned here with stating the essence of the reform program, down to its very last consequences. We will move on to look at the ideal of a stable price level and, subsequently, to the question as to whether or not the dangers inherent in the gold standard are sufficient to forbid a return to that standard, irrespective of this far-reaching aim and the resulting necessity to drop gold as the basis for our monetary system.

2

Even if fluctuations in the purchasing power of the monetary unit are considered to be an evil by those concerned (at all times and from all possible angles), they do not necessarily have to be considered only as a fault in the capitalist machine, nor does their function within its mechanism need to be denied. Only those fluctuations that are caused by the unpredictability of gold production can be justifiably considered pointless: the others cannot. Seasonal fluctuations, for example, are the very mechanism by which, on the one hand, the distribution of the annual product is implemented throughout the whole year and in which, on the other hand, the formation of expectations regarding production returns for the near future is expressed. Fluctuations in the price level that, given the composition of the general indices, can also originate from separate products or groups of products, hardly warrant a special apology. Secular falls in the price level, be they real or potential, that originate from commodities, are usually nothing other than the method by which the returns from progress in production are distributed over all classes of the population. Secular price rises in certain countries can be the result of overconsumption and the external expression of processes of impoverishment, often exerting extreme pressure to save. And finally, price fluctuations originating in national catastrophes, wars, revolutions, and so on, serve, in addition to the functions referred to above (and particularly when they take place under the pressure of inflation in paper money), to extract the last drop of strength and energy out of an industrial organism. This might not be fair, but at least it works very fast and effectively. They also make possible accomplishments that would otherwise have been out of question. In all of these cases, an appropriate credit policy can do a lot to alleviate the situation. Yet, there is always the danger that it will hamper the adaptation of the national economy to new circumstances, and, therefore, the question continues to arise: in which other way can this adaptation be achieved? The monetary and credit system might well be the immediate cause of the possible evil in all of these cases, but not the last one. And the method of reorganizing the finance and credit system, by dealing with the more deep-lying causes of the relevant disturbances, is, in most cases, more appropriate, more natural, and more effective than the reverse method of trying to eliminate these deeper causes through credit policy-oriented measures.[1]

The question of the price cycle within the trade cycle, therefore, still remains. It is, after all, this phenomenon which the monetary reformers tend to think of in the first instance, while the idea of complete stability of the price level is only defended as an extreme exception. One must remember two things, if one is not to be mistaken regarding the magnitude of this problem. In the first place, the disturbances in the economic lives of all peoples, which accompanied the postwar period, are not simply the result of a normal swing in the trade cycle. Unemployment, the loss of wealth, the collapse during the postwar period, are all an expression of the destruction caused by the war, the impoverishment of many countries, current social tensions, and the sudden necessity for all countries to adapt their industries to the production of goods for peace instead of war, and a very different type of peacetime production at that. The boom of 1920 and the ensuing crisis were the world economy's way of dealing with all this. I do not believe that it would have been an unmixed blessing if measures had been taken to prevent this, because credit policy would have made first the boom and then the ensuing depression impossible. No sensible person would, however, wish to deny that the normal principles of banking policy could not be applied under such circumstances. But all of this has nothing whatsoever to do with the mechanism of the normal trade cycle, as we knew it prior to the war, and one must not consider the catastrophes, losses, and damage of the past years as proof that the aforementioned, normal economic cycle was one of the greatest social ills. Certainly, prices also fall in normal periods of depression, but only by a small percentage, while, as we are well aware, the physical volume of the goods produced, transported, and traded only marginally decreases, as a rule. Certainly,

---

1. We have experienced an example of this in Austria. Here, the money system was first reorganized (i.e., the Austrian krone was stabilized in the hope that the rest would then fall into place). The result was a crisis of such a magnitude that the reorganization of the money system, which was in itself a success, appeared to be a failure, in retrospect.

the real wage falls below the level of the previous peak during a slump, but it does remain higher than prior to the preceding boom. And finally, unemployment figures during the worst period certainly tend to be four times as high as at the peak, but this level and the normal duration of this phenomenon are not such that unemployment insurance can be considered a hopelessly inadequate measure for softening the blow. In the past, we allowed ourselves to be influenced too much by the pessimistic mood that prevailed in the business community during the depression and we saw things much worse than they really were. In the second place, one must not forget that our monetary reformers are "doctoring" an evil here that has the tendency to "heal" if left alone. In this respect, too, one should not allow oneself to be misled by phenomena that are a consequence of the World War—no more than one might say, for example, that the events between 1914 and 1918 prove that mortality among the population of Europe is on the increase. We are all familiar with the type of crisis from the past, for example, that of 1873: the dramatic panics, the collapse that destroyed both good and bad firms at random, the situations that seemed both incomprehensible and hopeless to contemporaries, and the despair of the national institutions. This is all virtually a thing of the past. People understand the capitalist machine better. The banks are more aware of the nature and scope of their activities and the leading figures on the money market do not lose their heads as easily anymore. There are two more reasons why the depression of the future is bound to be less extreme and dangerous: in the first place, as a consequence of the movement toward concentration in industry and the financial world, economic life is becoming more subject to the control of large concerns that are so strong that no depression could threaten their existence and whose investment policy becomes independent of the economic situation at any given moment. Moreover, we are also, as we all know, well on our way toward acquiring such a precise knowledge of the trade cycle and obtaining such a finely detailed economic meteorology that even the most simple salesman will soon find it difficult to make a blunder, at least regarding those decisions that are based on the general economic situation. Just about everything that could be considered bad in the trade cycle is, in this way, neutralized.

While our monetary reformers are committing the original sin of all reformers, namely, by exaggerating the wrongs that need righting, they are making it all the easier for themselves, with their diagnosis of the sickness and the answer to the question as to whether or not what they want to cure is, in fact, a sickness. With particular precision, Hawtrey has referred to the economic swing as a purely monetary phenomenon. Similarly, Keynes has claimed that the changes in the variables K and K^1

in his equation (it seems to me more correct to speak simply of expansion and contraction of the extent of the bank money here) are the causes of the evil. That is to say: the credit policy of the banks is the sole cause of prosperity and depression. Expansion of credit encourages both good and bad firms alike, conjures up visions of profits through the price movements it has instigated, even if they do not already exist, and leads to an irrational expansion of production and speculative excesses. Contraction of credit, which, moreover, occurs merely as a consequence of the necessity to exchange bank deposits for legal currency, therefore makes an end to all of this; both far too late and far too drastically, puts pressure on the price level; brings both good and bad enterprises to a standstill, and induces unemployment; a completely pointless state of affairs, therefore, an unadulterated ill, which must clearly be combatted by means of a banking policy as soon as the opportunity to do so presents itself. In his speech at the annual meeting of the Royal Economic Society in June, 1924, Keynes challenged his opponents to say precisely how far they agreed with this diagnosis.

I consider it to be incorrect. Not because I doubt that economic fluctuations can be averted through credit policy. Nor because I query the proposition that the rise in price level during a period of prosperity and its fall during a depression is directly caused by monetary events. But simply because I am of the opinion that both prosperity and depression fulfill an essential role and that, in turn, expansion and contraction of credit are important "actors," very difficult to replace. In other words: it is not Keynes's monetary theory that I contest, but his theory of the trade cycle.

What characterizes a period of prosperity is not simply an increased level of activity and more widespread speculation that runs the normal course. The essence of the phenomenon is to be found more in the taking of a new course. New men with new objectives appear, the productive forces of the national economy are combined into new industrial and commerical opportunities, into new production layouts and production methods. The new things mostly take shape within new enterprises; they do not necessarily emerge from their closely-related predecessors, but arise alongside and in competition. For every boom known to economic history, it is possible to point to sectors of manufacturing, to production methods, to organizational arrangements, and so on, that led to their development. This also provides an explanation for the increased number of newly founded enterprises and the rise in investments during periods of boom, factors that feature, to a greater or lesser degree, in most modern theories on the trade cycle. That industrial progress is not an even process over time, that, on the contrary, the decisive steps are concentrated periodically in a short space of time, can be explained quite simply: it is very difficult, both technically and psychologically, to undertake something new, but, once initial success has been achieved and the path becomes clear, all technical and financial risks and psychological barriers within the business and financial world tend to diminish. The meaning and function of periods of prosperity in a capitalist society is, therefore, the partial change of course in the national economy, toward new objectives, a change in the distribution of the available forces of production, and a periodical reorganization of manufacturing; the meaning and function of periodical slumps is the absorption and processing of what has been newly created through the normal cycle. As every period of prosperity involves a limited number of new perspectives, the incentive tends to lose its impetus within a few years, and as the new is subject to practical restrictions each time, the depression has done its work within a few years. A period of boom is, therefore, a typical deviation from the reality of the static picture of economic organization, a depression the epitomization of the tendency that reality displays to return toward a stable equilibrium.

The role that the monetary and credit system and the fluctuations in the price level (which clearly have a monetary basis) play here, becomes clear when one sets them against the normal state of a static economy. In the static cycle, complete parallelism exists, in principle, between the flow of goods and money. The fruits of productive activities or the capitalization of previously produced products provide all economic subjects with sums of money that they then spend on the commodities market, whereby these sums return to the producers, who then spend them on the means of production market. The sums that appear on the commodities market within a certain period, on the one hand, and those that arise on the production market on the other, are not merely similar, but identical. In essence, it is a question of the uninterrupted exchange of products for means of production; money and credit have no other function here than to facilitate payments; they do not exercise any influence on economic activity. Whatever else happens in this cycle with respect to the extension of credit merely belongs to the category of circulating credit. Every unit of purchasing power represents a certain quantity of consumer goods—and precisely those that can be purchased by force of habit—and, at the same time, a certain amount of productive activity, which, in turn, ripens into consumer goods during the economic period in question. This would be the situation if there was no such thing as economic development: the production process would be continually financed by the funds from previous production. However, when businesses previously unknown to the trade cycle emerge, or if completely new enterprises are established, new production methods introduced, and so on, then such resources from the capitalization of the results of previous production periods are not, generally, available. They are, therefore, dependent on credit, and not on credit in the form that this can take in the static cycle and in which it fulfills merely a market-technical function in the circulation sphere, but in a completely different and more essential sense. We are confronted here with the most prominent example of the need for credit in capitalist society. It is the only case in which credit is basically indispensable, and necessary in any description of the events.

In order to satisfy this need for credit, annual savings could, in the first instance, be made available. In as far as the new syndicates emerge from already-existing concerns, the previous and not-yet-distributed returns of the latter are available, after all. In these cases, it is purely a question of the relevant sums, which should have entered first the market for producer goods and then the market for consumer goods, being used in a different way than usual, without a notable increase in the total demand. However, it is a different matter if the new need for investment is met with sums that were not circulating previously. New purchasing power, to which no new goods initially correspond, emerges alongside the old and pushes the price level up. This can happen if sums of money that, in a given country, had not previously circulated at all or at least not in the normal cycle of production and consumption, now start to appear, for example, through foreign credit or by the mobilization of reserves (of whatever kind) of the capital market. The most important and most interesting possibility, however, is simply the expansion of bank credit, whereby new purchasing power is created out of nothing. In this case, it is also unimportant when the new purchasing power, from the point of view of the circulation process, also emerges from nothing, however securely the credit might be assured by property items not destined for circulation, in just the same way as the state of reserve is, in itself, immaterial and of a purely psychological significance for the inflationary effects of a bank note issue. Of course, credit further expands once the process is under way, due to speculative anticipation. The reverse applies in periods of depression and results in this: the new investments create products, or everyone expects them, so that afterwards the parallelism between money and commodities shows a tendency toward recovery. Furthermore, if the new investments reap normal success, the credit extended during the boom will gradually find its way back to the investor. A mood of pessimism enters the circles of vested interest threatened by the new competition and there is further contraction of credit, based on this and on speculative anticipation. All of these forces lead to a fall in prices during the slump.

In the first place, this analysis therefore confirms the views of the reformers, that the credit policy pursued by the banks is the immediate cause of the price cycle and, thereby, also of many other phenomena in the trade cycle. It is also clear that by taking similar credit policy measures, for example, by a credit-expanding and credit-contracting neutralizing modification of the circulation of bank notes—the discount policy alone would not be sufficient here—such fluctuations in the price level can, accordingly, be averted. It is equally evident that this would not only result in the simple elimination of a fault in the credit machine, but that a part of this machine, so essential to the national economy, would be paralyzed. Because it is these temporary deviations from the parallelism between the flow of goods and the means of circulation, this periodic inflation and deflation of credit, that constitute the very method by which the economic organization of economic progress, resting on private property, competition, and credit, is conducted and its results become absorbed into the normal cycle. Both aspects of the trade cycle are, indeed, necessary here. The inflation of credit during a period of prosperity diverts, through the rise in price level that it causes, part of the available means of production from the targets to which they had been consigned so far, and makes them available for new men and new goals. If one wished to dismiss this process, then one would have to be consistent in preventing the import of foreign capital, which has, broadly speaking, the same purpose. Both the relative and absolute deflation of credit during a slump not only restores the normal relation between commodities and circulation. The very fall in price that it causes leads, on the one hand, to a rise in the real income of consumers, thereby allowing the whole population to taste the fruits of the boom. On the other hand, it casts aside the superseded, thereby realizing the achievements of the boom for the structure of production of the national economy. This whole process, and the aforementioned rejection of what has been superseded, in particular, does not occur without shocks. Neither does it take place in the ideal manner. The uncertainty regarding the ultimate success of the new and its effects on the old (and, therefore, on all economic factors) that reigns during the course of this process of absorption, which in turn constitutes the essence of the slump, means that while much of the old and antiquated survives, given adequate support, much of what is healthy and vigorous perishes. The precautionary measures taken on all sides lead to temporary restrictions of production and, thereby, to a higher increase in unemployment than necessary.

An argument in favor of a more discriminating crisis therapy would therefore not be completely unjustified. But an attack on the fundaments of the whole process would, given this state of affairs, serve to check economic progress, unless accompanied by many more reforms in the capitalist economy.

Conclusion

If one is, therefore, of the opinion that a society should first possess those institutions capable of assuming the roles now fulfilled by fluctuations in the price level, then the basic grounds for rejecting the principles of old banking policy and, thereby, also for a release from the gold standard, no longer apply. As it is quite clear that while the world is slowly beginning to recover from the ruptures and decline of the war, and while international cooperation is still difficult and hazardous, there are other more urgent worries than dealing with the problems associated with the fluctuations in gold production. The practical question of the return to gold is, therefore, restricted to the dangers and problems that one might anticipate with respect to the present gold situation. A return to the gold standard is understood in the widest sense here: we do not mean, for example, purely establishing a relationship between monetary units and quantities of gold, nor merely gold-based systems, but rather tha actual holding of gold reserves and, if possible, the effective circulation of gold, even if only indirectly. It is only in this way that the majority of the benefits provided by the gold standard, and the degree of automatism in particular, can be guaranteed, as is the case with the free gold monetary systems (to their continuing credit). This is despite all arguments from the monetary reformers and despite all necessity to support the value of gold in the present circumstances. The return to the gold standard has nothing to do with deflation, as the relation on the grounds of which this return takes place is essentially arbitrary. Without being able to go into more detail here, I would like to say that the same thing appears to be happening here as so often occurs in our discipline: following a period in which the typically and imprudently obstinate idea of the "sound money man," with interest only for the old parity, is contested with very convincing arguments, one has now, luckily, overshot the mark. And to such an extent that even those arguments that could have potentially supported the old parity are now more or less subject to contempt. However, even a return to the old parity at the expense of a certain level of deflation can sometimes be worth recommending. Not just a return, but a speedy one, which makes an end to the long detours and seemingly endless uncertainty, which is often responsible for all the disadvantages and suffering that people try to blame on the deflationary policy as such.

The problem with the present gold situation is not to be found in the increase in the world supply of monetary gold. This has hardly increased by more than two billion dollars since 1914 and would not even be sufficient to provide a gold circulation of prewar dimensions, given the current price level, which no one would like to see fall sharply. This is also the reason why an effective circulation of gold would probably only be possible after a number of years and why the caution that characterises England's present attitude is fully justifiable. There lurks no danger in that one billion of gold that the European central banks have on balance in excess of the prewar period, and even less so in the gold that is to be found in America beyond the Treasury and the Federal Reserve Banks. The only danger is in the American reserve. This is almost three times as high as in peacetime, and would certainly be sufficient, when applied according to the old principles, to raise American prices to double the present level if the American central institutions were, for whatever reason, willing to abandon their current policies. Those countries that had linked their monetary system to gold before such an event were to happen would be dragged along in this unparalleled boom, and equally in the ensuing crisis. And even if things did not turn out as badly as that, and the American central institutions eased (if not fully, then at least partially) the brake, then those European countries that had adopted the gold standard would still be dependent on the insight of the American leadership for their economic well-being. This is the basis of the argument put forward by monetary reformers on this point.

I am not saying that Keynes is seeing ghosts. The gold situation cannot, of course, be relaxed without problems, and particularly not without deviating from the old principles of banking policy, although the problems are, in reality, of a smaller magnitude than he would have us believe. A modest increase in the American price level would be enough to cause a flow of goods to the United States. This would make it easier for Europe to overcome its crisis and fulfill its obligations, while for America it would mean a realization of its accumulated wealth. In the meantime, the question is: how will American politics deal with this goods flow? It is more difficult here to rely on a prudent attitude than with respect to the gold situation or banking policy alone. It is perfectly possible that the ingrained protectionist slogans would still predominate and that new import bans would be introduced to block this healthy method of economic detente. It is here that the real danger lies, and not in credit policy. But America will sooner or later have to get used to the role of creditor state with a passive trade balance, whether it likes it or not. Even earlier, its greatly enlarged production apparatus will be increasingly emphasizing the importance of exports. Such a development assumes, however, unrestricted import. Both of these forces must persist; the question is merely when. A policy of free trade in America is, as it were, the real cure for the present situation; not only for the gold situation. This, too, will be relaxed in a natural way, as America is freed from the pressure of excess gold and Europe's return to the gold standard is facilitated. The European central banks will only have to adopt the present American banking policy during those periods in which this gold is actually flowing in.

Furthermore, America realizes its wealth through the export of capital. The resulting expansion of its economic sphere of power is the unavoidable consequence of the economic shifts during wartime. Considering that this export of capital must, in the final instance and given the present state of affairs, take the form of gold exports, then the one or two billion of American gold that is causing our monetary reformers such headaches will probably be drained away more quickly than anyone expects or hopes for. And it is toward this outflow or this appropriation of gold, perhaps even toward a large transaction for the recovery of European currency systems, that the American gold policy is geared. The attempt to avoid gold inflation is certainly also a motive, although to expect America to demonetize gold would be a complete misinterpretation of its banking policy. It is clearly a question of maintaining the monetary role of gold and the prospect of doing well after a return to gold. Far from viewing the basic principles that the Federal Reserve Board used to determine its policy over the past few years as an essential steering away from gold, be it intentional or unintentional, the whole point of the policy was to divert it back to gold.

This line of thought leads one to the conclusion that the dangers and problems of a return to the gold standard are exaggerated by the reformers. The arguments on the general benefits of the gold standard, of the consideration for the vested interests (and in particular for the issuing banks), and the arguments on the relative simplicity, the comprehensibility, and the ease of reorganizing finance inherent in a return to gold, speak for themselves. But this is not the decisive factor, as far as we are concerned. If one takes a good look at our whole line of reasoning, then one will see, at every step, that the return to gold is not merely an effective measure in monetary terms. Gold and its movement provides, in the very extent to which this is automatic or can again become so (and on the very road toward this), the most effective mechanism available at present for solving a number of nonmonetary economic, political, and social problems. The free gold standard could help Europe to overcome its crisis, could help America to get used to its new position, could bring peoples closer together, could enforce peaceful cooperation on pain of immediately felt economic losses, could aid groups of disadvantaged workers in their fight for better living conditions, and much more. Even if the gold standard is not an ideal, in itself, how can people seek to reject it right at this moment, when it is about to do mankind a great— and perhaps final—service?

Commentary

Mark Perlman

It is best to start with the appendix to this paper, the appendix being an article by Schumpeter, originally printed in the Dutch language in 1925. It had been delivered earlier that year as a Netherlands School of Economics lecture, presumably in German. In it, Schumpeter lays out (1) his immediate differences with Maynard Keynes about the wisdom of Britain's return to the gold standard; (2) his profound philosophical differences about priorities relating to the short and the long haul in economics; and (3) his developed despair about his own ability to control governmental intervention.

Van Paridon does great service to the profession by resurrecting this article, outlining the line of argument and the differences in perspective of the two men, and particularly for suggesting, if only faintly, an explanation for the temperamental and political differences between them, as well as assessing the article's role in the development of the discipline.

What Schumpeter has principally in mind, to refer to the Keynesian literature, is Keynes's proclivity to concentrate on the short haul—to put the matter in Keynes's words: "In the long run we are all dead. Economists set themselves too easy, too useless a task if in tempestuous seasons they can only tell us that when the storm is long past the ocean is flat again" ([1923] 1971, 65). Schumpeter, at heart something of an institutional economic historian, thinks that the underlying historico-economic forces cannot be successfully muffled over long periods of time, and that a scholarly assessment of the usual pattern of economic development is to recognize that change is both inevitable and painful.

But there is something else. When Schumpeter wrote his book on the history of economic dogma (buried from the profession by the outbreak of World War I), what he offered was a panegyric of the Consultant Administrator. By the time he wrote this paper, he had had his chance and he had failed. Personally disillusioned, he generalized on his own experience. In the 1920s, he was eager to repudiate his earlier enthusiasm and to use this attack on Keynes's policies to repudiate the principle of a disinterested intellectual reshaping the economy for the good of the social order. As an aside, I suggest that Keynes's dominant role at the 1944 Bretton Woods conference must have been well-aged bitter wormwood and gall to Schumpeter.

What the van Paridon paper does not treat, which I think it should have, is (1) the intellectual nature and degree of the Rotterdam criticism of the Schumpeter thesis, and also (2) what was involved in Schumpeter's compulsive choosing of abrasive rhetoric on so many occasions where he was a guest speaker. In the twenties, he even allowed himself to be abrasive in print; something that I think he came to abandon in his last works, the *History* as well as the later essays on Great Economists. True, he had the earlier experience of alienating his one-time sponsor, Eugen von Böhm-Bawerk, which may have been the latter's fault as much as his own, but what Schumpeter was doing in Rotterdam was not only sticking it to Keynes, but, in handling the matter the way he did, he seems to have chosen to make an enemy where he could have made something of an ally. After all, Keynes was no socialist, and as van Paridon has pointed out, Koopmans, who was a socialist, immediately seems to have come to Keynes's defense, not for the love of Keynes, but for the hatred of Schumpeter. Schumpeter set out to be a double loser–a posture that he came to master.

At the point when he wrote this paper, Schumpeter's opposition to Keynes was, I think, mostly a framing problem. That is, as I have already suggested, Schumpeter's preference for long-haul versus short-haul analysis. Besides that, he was aware of Keynes's tendency to imperial British autarkic solutions, which offended Schumpeter's own preference for free trade. One can, I think, argue with ease that his later disagreements with Keynes stretched to cover differing views about the productive or counterproductive role of state fiscal intervention. I am not aware of the precise differences he had with Keynes's contributions to the economic theory of uncertainty, but I suspect that there was no personal bridge in this area, either.

Schumpeter, among others, pointed out that the Menger-Schmoller *Methodenstreit* was not a fight about method, but a fight about free trade. By way of relative comparison, I wonder whether the constant fights that Schumpeter had were not policy questions, but simply personal vanities. About ten years ago, I asked Don Moggridge to look for any Keynes-Schumpeter correspondence in the Keynes papers. He found only one. Schumpeter had made a luncheon date with Keynes in Cambridge, had arrived very late, and Keynes (ever the British gentleman) had stayed his own lunch until Schumpeter arrived. Schumpeter wrote a combined letter of apology and thanks. After reading the letter, and knowing, myself, something about the warmth, yet implicit superiority, of Keynes's personal manner, I inferred that much as Schumpeter might not have been stymied by Keynes's suave, if exaggerated, savoir faire (something of a match between two masters, that), he had real reason to envy Keynes's institutional security. Keynes, never a professor, enjoyed far more aura than any Harvard professor possessed. The *Economic Journal,* as well as the *New Statesman,* to say nothing of the institution of letters to the *Times,* gave Keynes a public that Schumpeter must have envied. And while Harvard's Taussig, too, had a journal (one older than Keynes's *Economic Journal* and certainly in the same prestigious class), Taussig never could throw his opinions around as quickly and powerfully as Keynes did—if for no other reasons than that Taussig's more ponderous thinking process took far more time, and Taussig lacked a taste for blood. Obviously, Taussig and Schumpeter were the closest of friends, but Schumpeter (unlike Taussig, and like Keynes) seems to me to have had something of a taste for blood.

Or to put the matter more simply, if partly erroneously, I mentioned to Claude Jessua yesterday that the Schumpeter who wrote *Capitalism, Socialism and Democracy* had every known reason to be bitter about what life had, in the end, dealt out to him. But part of the reason that his life was so bitter is that he could not be generous to his equals. Many men are kind to their juniors (and that Schumpeter surely was); his trouble was that he had a dueler's instinct for blood. And this is just another example of a man intent upon pursuing the road to loneliness, loneliness of person and paucity of immediate influence.

REFERENCES

Moggridge, Donald, ed. 1971. *The Collected Writings of John Maynard Keynes.* Vol. IV, *A Tract on Monetary Reform.* London: The Macmillan Press Ltd.

Contributors

Jürgen G. Backhaus, Department of Economics, University of Limburg

Laurence S. Moss, Department of Economics, Babson College

C. W. A. M. van Paridon, Scientific Council for Government Policy, The Netherlands

Mark Perlman, Department of Economics, University of Pittsburgh

Nathan Rosenberg, Department of Economics, Stanford University

Yuichi Shionoya, Professor of Economics and President Emeritus, Hitotsubashi University

Erich Streissler, Department of Economics, University of Vienna

Shigeto Tsuru, Professor of Economics Emeritus and President Emeritus, Hitotsubashi University, Tokyo

Kiichiro Yagi, Faculty of Economics, Kyoto University

Index

Knies, Carl, 24–26, 31, 33, 40
knowledge, 48, 51
Koopmans, J. G., 100–101, 126
Krelle, Wilhelm, 104
"Krise der Steuerstaates, Die" 2, 6,
    67
Krüger, Kersten, 67
Kyoto University Economic Review, 6

Laffer, Arthur, 82
Laffer curve, 82
Lambers, Hendrik W., 96, 100
Lancaster, K., 59
Lange, Oskar, 6, 9, 61
Lederer, Emil, 30
Leibenstein, Harvey, 75
Leser, Norbert, 22
Liefmann, Robert, 27–28, 33
Lindahl, 65–66

management, 11, 17–18, 31
Mangoldt, 17
Marshall, Alfred, 18, 36, 78, 113
Marshallian economics, 48
Marx, Karl, 12, 20, 30, 40, 54–56, 75
Marxian reproduction scheme, 5
Marxian school, 11, 15, 30, 36, 39,
    103
März, Eduard, 23, 27
Mataja, Viktor, 21
Means, Gardiner C., 31
Menger, Carl, 14, 16, 19, 21, 24, 27,
    36, 38
mercantilism, 15, 97, 112
"methodenstreit," 37–38, 126
"methodological individualism," 3,
    26n.50, 40
Milgate, M., 61
Mill, John Stuart, 22–24, 54
Mises, Ludwig von, 30, 36–37, 60–61
Moddridge, Donald, 126
Mohr, J. C. B., 17
monopoly, 10, 11, 14–15, 21, 26–29,
    30, 32–33, 46–47, 72n.8, 83–84,
    87–88

Morgan, Theodore, 5
Moss, Laurence, 3
Mun, Thomas, 15–16
Musgrave, Richard A., 2, 65, 67

Naderer, Bärbel, 102
Nelson, Richard R., 45–46
Neo-Austrian school, 15, 36–37
neoclassical economics, 2, 3, 27, 41–
    44, 46–48, 50–51, 54, 61
Netherlands School of Economics, 96
neutrality of money, 101
Newton, Isaac, 44
Nietzsche, Friedrich, 13–14

O'Connor, James, 67
ownership, 10–11, 98–99

Pareto, Vilfredo, 74, 77, 83
Pareto principle, 75
path-dependency, 56
Perlman, Mark, 3, 104
Physiocrats, 52
Posthuma, S., 96, 100
privatization, 2, 8–11
profit, 16, 84, 87–88, 98, 117
property rights, 63, 84, 98–99, 109,
    113, 120
Prussian revenue system, 69
public expenditure. *See* public
    finance
public finance, 2, 3, 65–91

Quesnay, François, 12

Rathenau, W., 96
rational expectations, 49
rationality, 47–50, 53, 62, 117
Rau, Karl Heinrich, 16–18, 24, 39
Ricardian economics, 103
Ricardo, David, 22, 37, 67
Riedel, A. F., 19–22, 26, 36, 39
Rimpler, 71
Romer, Paul M., 20
Roscher, Wilhelm, 18–19, 24, 26